WE SWAM THE GRAND CANYON

WE SWAM THE GRAND CANYON

BILL BEER

THE MOUNTAINEERS/SEATTLE

*The Mountaineers: Organized 1906 to
". . . explore, study, preserve, and enjoy the natural beauty of the outdoors."*

© 1988 by Bill Beer
All rights reserved

21098
54321

Published by The Mountaineers
306 2nd Avenue West, Seattle, Washington 98119

Published simultaneously in Canada
By Douglas & McIntyre Ltd.
1615 Venables St., Vancouver, British Columbia V5L 2H1

Manufactured in the United States of America

*Edited by Jenny Keller
Designed by Marjorie Mueller
Cover design by Elizabeth Watson
Map by Debbie Newell
Photos by the author and John Daggett*

Library of Congress Cataloging-in-Publication Data

Beer, Bill, 1929-
    We swam the Grand Canyon : the true story of a cheap vacation that got a little out of hand / by Bill Beer.
      p. cm.
    ISBN 0-89886-151-9 :
    1. Beer, Bill, 1929- . 2. Swimmers—United States—Biography.
3. Swimming, Long distance—Colorado River. 4. Grand Canyon (Ariz.)—Description and travel. I. Title.
GV838.B39A3 1988
797.2'1'0922—dc19
[B]
                                                                      88-5378
                                                                         CIP

For Barrie & Ben,
who asked for this book

and, of course, John
(who probably would have written a better one)

Contents

1
"Watch Out, Mister" 15

2
Rapids, Icewater and Fire 31

3
Getting in Deeper 49

4
Blood and Fear 67

5
The Big Canyon 85

6
Caught in the Act 101

7
"This River Is Out to Get Me" 115

8
Lava Falls and Burro Meat 135

9
Lost . . . and Found! 151

Aftermath 161

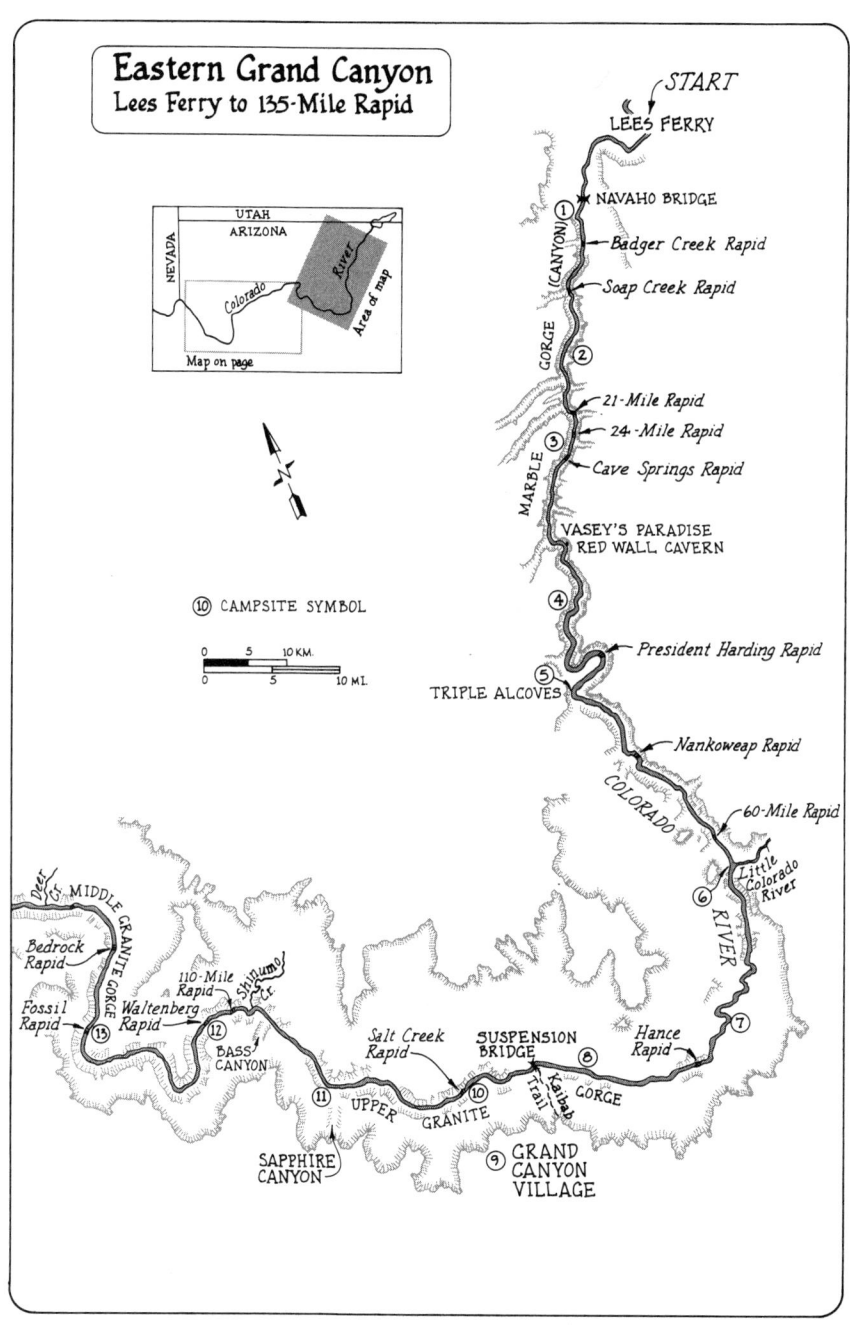

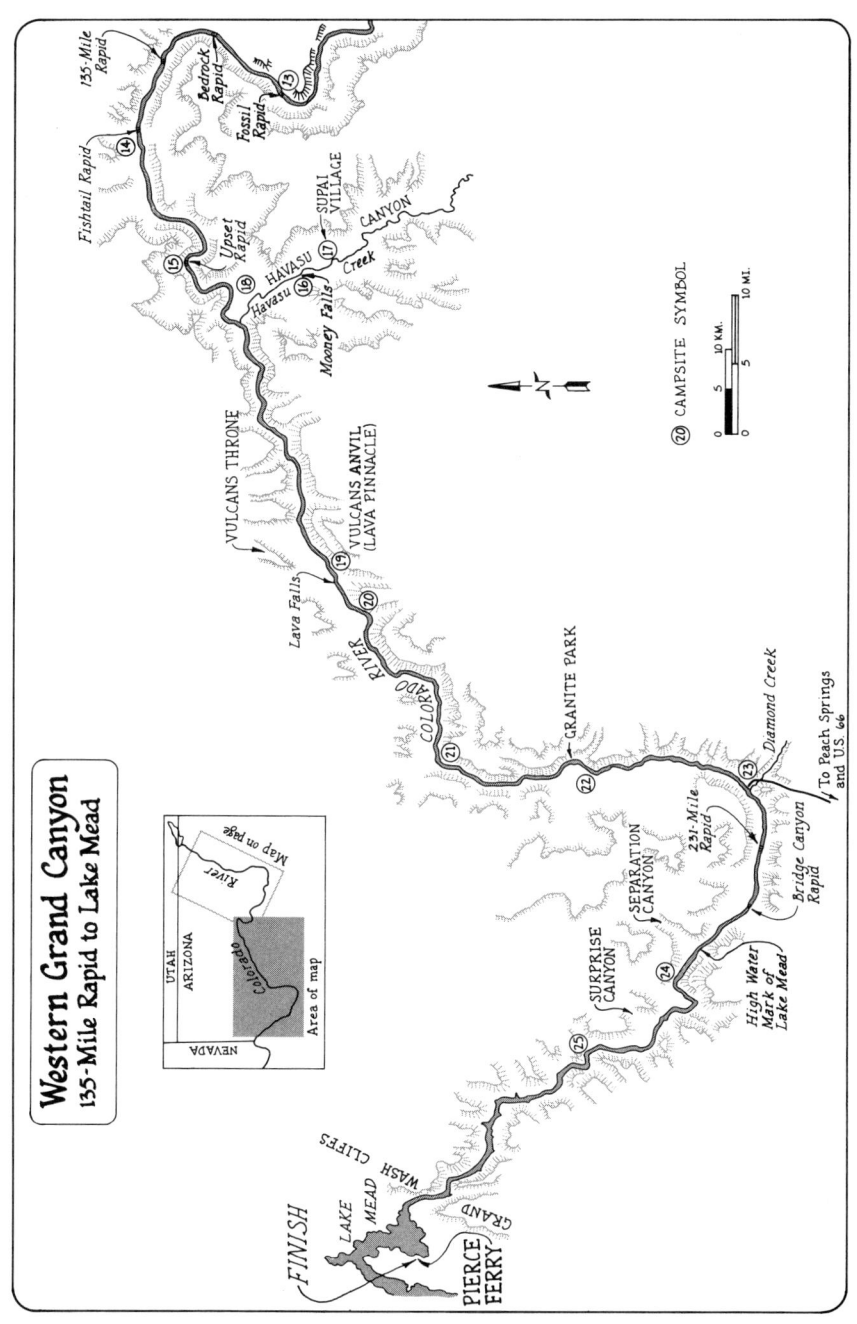

WE SWAM THE GRAND CANYON

1

Watch Out, Mister

The noise nearly overwhelmed us. The cold, dirty river thundered down its gorge with a roar like a train going through a tunnel. And in the late afternoon isolation of the Grand Canyon there seemed to be only us . . . and all that noise.

Standing on the boulders below the thousand-foot cliffs staring at the rapid we had our first serious doubts. Or fears?

"Do you want to go first?" John yelled.

"Not particularly," I shouted back.

"Then I will," he declared rather more quietly and proceeded to give me detailed instructions on where I should set up our camera for the best coverage. Normally, I would have insisted on discussing the merits of several locations, but this seemed to be his show.

Orders given, John turned and began to clamber upstream over the boulders making a narrow path between cliff and river.

Left alone with the little movie camera and the noise, I wondered whether John really could swim through this savage rapid. We had been months planning for and working toward this moment, but now that it was here it all seemed so unreal, as if someone else were here, not me.

John was gone, out of sight. If something happened to him, if he got hurt or killed, I might not even know about it. And if I did know, what could I do to help . . . if anything? Staring up at the sheer, vertical rock cliffs, I wondered how I would get out of here if the whole thing were a bust?

We were 11 miles out on our planned 280-mile swim of the Colorado River through Marble Gorge and the Grand Canyon. It was early April, 1955, and at that time only about 200 people had traveled this stretch in boats—none, of course, had swum it. We were in the prime of youth and this river adventure had seemed like great fun. Since we couldn't afford a boat and all the necessary equipment, we had conceived the idea of going without a boat. Swimming the Colorado? Why not?

John Daggett and I had been friends for the eight years since we were sophomore roommates at Stanford, during which time we had kept in touch more or less regularly. After we both got out of the military and after his wife and children had been killed in a terrible accident, we roomed together again and shared a few activities. Both of us had done some surfing and were used to rough waters. We were good swimmers and in very good condition. Not any better, mind you, than thousands of other young men on beaches all over the world. But we did have more than our share of imagination, I suppose.

And so it was that one rainy January day in 1955 we were in our apartment spinning fantasies—this time about rivers and rapids and their legendary dangers—with a friend who had had some experience. We were pooh-poohing the self-made heroics of our friend and others when, in a burst of bravado, John declared that we could *swim* the Colorado, the biggest and toughest of the U.S. rivers.

The room was suddenly silent. The idea lay there glowing, and pulsing, and hypnotizing us with its possibilities.

Then just as suddenly the room was full of words as we expanded, enthused, explored and tried to find flaws in the idea.

"We could get killed."

"Nah, guys have accidentally swum rapids and lived; we'll do it better on purpose."

"And it can't be any rougher than body surfing around rocks along the Pacific Coast."

"Nobody's even tried anything like that, have they?"

"Have you ever *seen* the Colorado River?"

"Never."

"How many rapids does it have?"

"Lots!"

"It sure would be a blast!"

"Boy, I bet some people would be really upset."

"Who?"

"You know. All those guys who think they're so hot."

"And the Government?"

"They'd probably stop us."

"Not if they didn't know!"

After a few visits to the Los Angeles Public Library we had all we could get on the subject of the Colorado River and its voyagers.

The river itself is the third longest system in the U.S., draining one-twelfth of the country. Sixteen hundred miles long, it starts high in the Rocky Mountains and drops two and a half miles in its roaring charge to the desert, carving out over a dozen major canyon systems. The largest and longest of these is the 280-mile-long, mile-deep Marble Gorge Grand Canyon system.

Discovered by Europeans only 48 years after Columbus' first voyage, it was not until after the Civil War, in 1869, that the first trip through the Grand Canyon was made. Part of the reason is that the

Grand Canyon system is dug into the heart of some of the most wild and inaccessible country in the U.S. A famous remark made by Lieutenant Joseph Ives after his official expedition through the area in 1858 was that "Ours has been the first, and will doubtless be the last, party of whites to visit this profitless locality. It seems intended by nature that the Colorado River, along the greater portion of its lonely and majestic way, shall be forever unvisited and undisturbed."*

Standing alone on my rock at Soap Creek Rapid waiting for John, I knew things had improved since 1858, but the chances of our getting any help if we needed it were still on a par with Lieutenant Ives' chances. About zero. So John would be very slow and careful getting ready, leaving me time to reflect on some of the things we had learned about the river and its rapids.

In the 86 years since Major John Wesley Powell's pioneer trip only 30 plus groups had actually completed a trip through the Grand Canyon. Surveyors, map makers, geologists, trappers and just plain adventurers had tried the trip with varying success. Wooden boats, metal boats, and more recently, rubber boats had been used — a fair number of which had been wrecked and abandoned.

The rapids were thought to be the most dangerous feature of the river; in fact, it was not until 1938 that a man was able to claim that he had run them all. Until then, and for years after, most people carried their boats around the biggest rapids. No one had tried it without a boat, though most of those thrown out of their boats had survived.

What little swimming had been done, accidentally or otherwise, had added to the legends. A half dozen or so widely publicized drownings on those expeditions had given the river a bad name. Considering the few people who ventured on the river it

---

*Later, the prescient Ives joined the Confederate Army.

was a heavy toll, and swimming in the river came to be considered an invitation to death. In the Grand Canyon where the Park Service had jurisdiction, swimming in the Colorado was actually prohibited.

The information available to us was sketchy at best, unreliable at worst. Different writers seemed to encounter different "perils." One would digress on the terrible quicksands of the Grand Canyon, while another would warn of the whirlpools or the heat. One party might have had great difficulties in a particular rapid, another scarcely noted the same rapid. "These guys ought to get together and read each other's books," remarked John.

With no dams upstream from the Grand Canyon, the river's maximum flood was sometimes 20 times its minimum flow — accounting at least for some of the variety in the descriptions of the rapids. Also, some writers complained bitterly of the cold water; others enjoyed tepid baths. We needed information, but really didn't want to advertise our plans by asking too many questions, so we wrote an innocuous letter to the measuring station the government maintains at Lees Ferry, Arizona, asking about water volume and temperature for various times of the year.

There is really only one logical place to start a trip through the Grand Canyon, Lees Ferry. But a finish point seemed not so easy. We learned that the Grand Canyon ends abruptly at the Grand Wash Cliffs and that the Colorado pours out of a gap in these cliffs into Lake Mead. In times of high water on the lake it stretches a long finger into the lower Grand Canyon. This presents little problem to those having boats with oars and motors, but if we found the lake extending into the canyons we would run out of current in a spot where we couldn't easily or safely get out and go home. And we didn't relish the thought of slowly swimming 50 or 60 miles of lake, towing our gear through the water just to find a place to get out.

The best we could do was find a place on a road map called Pierce Ferry, which seemed to give access to the river by road. Strip maps of the river and contour maps of the Grand Canyon were available from the Geological Survey, and these we ordered.

As January became February and then March, more and more of our time began to be spent on the project. We discussed it endlessly, trading ideas and bits of knowledge and testing out theories on each other. John's initial rush of enthusiasm began to fade in time while I became more and more convinced that we had a good plan and a good theory. The more I learned, the more convinced I became that we could do it and the more I was able to bolster John's enthusiasm. Soon he was again as optimistic as he had been at the beginning, leaving me in turn no room to weaken. This process of feeding on each other's confidence can be dangerous—a slow motion game of "chicken" leading to foolish ventures. We were safe enough as long as we kept the idea secret; we could back out without looking too foolish. And we had agreed on total secrecy, partly so as not to warn the authorities.

But one night at a party of friends John seized on a lull in the conversation to announce loudly, "Hey everybody, Bill and I are going to swim down the Colorado! Tell 'em, Bill."

Polite laughter.

"No really, we've got it all worked out." And the irrepressible John Daggett was off and running, easily convincing all who knew him that he was dead serious. Of course, everyone there had something to add. One had just returned from Lake Mead and told us we'd freeze to death; another was so convinced we'd die in the rapids he proposed to take out a life insurance policy on us. The consensus was that we were insane. But of course this just made us more determined.

About the middle of March the letter from Lees Ferry came. The river would likely be flooded, it said, from mid May to late July. We were afraid to tackle the river in flood stage, but the water temperature in April was predicted to be a cold 59 degrees. That left August and a much warmer 77-degree estimate.

"I guess we've got to wait another four months," said John.

"Watch Out, Mister"

It seemed that way, but I had a strong feeling that a four-month delay would kill the whole plan and it would become just another crazy scheme that never got out of the talk stage. Our momentum would be lost. There had to be a way to defeat either the cold water or the flood or we would see the idea die aborning.*

Again we didn't want to ask too many questions of the authorities or the experts for fear of revealing our intentions, so we chose to avoid the flood and face the cold water. Suits had been developed to protect scuba divers against even arctic waters, and they would have solved the problem, but at the time they were out of our price range—a boat would have been as cheap.

One day in a dive shop I found some thin rubber shirts on sale for $15 apiece. These, and a pair of woolen long john underwear became our bargain cold weather swimming gear. But how were we going to carry out supplies? Anything that even resembled a boat was out; a boat had become almost an impure thought. Inner tubes seemed impractical. Then a lucky find in a surplus shop solved that problem. There in a dusty corner lay some clumsy, misshapen rubber boxes. Designed to carry WWII radio gear and keep it dry under the worst conditions of swamp warfare, they were made of tough corded neoprene, could be sealed watertight, and held about three cubic feet of stuff. Best of all, they were only 89 cents each!

Two of these apiece would hold sleeping bags, cooking gear, and enough canned and dried food for a month. And even when filled, they floated.

Part of what John must have been doing now upstream at the beginning of Soap Creek Rapid was working out some way to get himself and his two heavy boxes through the rapid at the same

---

*I don't know why flood stage scared us—low water is probably more dangerous because the river is nearly as fast, but the rapids are shallower and rockier.

time. In the first 11 calm miles of river, which included one medium-sized rapid, we had both experimented with various ideas: towing the boxes, swimming alongside them with or without a lanyard attached, and just letting them float beside us. But none of those experiments had been in the raging waters of a big rapid. What had worked in calmer water could result here in loss of our supplies or worse.

Our basic premise, at this point untried, for successfully swimming rapids was simply that if the water flowed over and around the rocks, so would something floating in it. Unlike the driftwood and logs we found so many of in the river, we were flexible and would flow better. In addition, we could swim somewhat — using mostly our swim fins — and could perhaps steer away from trouble much as many of the oar-powered boats had before us.

Besides, weren't most boulders and rocks in a river worn round and smooth by millions of years of erosion? So if not soft, at least the rocks would be slippery and forgiving. Wouldn't they? But here at the edge of Soap Creek Rapids, and at the one or two places where we had already gotten out of the cold water, we had discovered to our dismay that many of the rocks at the edge of the Colorado were worn into knife-edge sharpness. We couldn't see those under the muddy water, but could guess.

Back in L.A. it had all seemed so simple. With the cat out of the bag, friends began calling us and asking pointed questions about our planned swim. Our glib answers had made it all seem so easy to us. We were on a track we couldn't be derailed from; each answer we gave to each objection merely reinforced our confidence. And if we didn't have a ready answer, we often made up one, which then became the truth to us. Friends began to seriously try to talk us out of it; they really did think we were going to die. We thought that preposterous.

April arrived. We set our departure for the tenth. We planned a trip of three weeks and bought food enough to last for about 24

"Watch Out, Mister"

days. Our stuff just fit into our space, but then some friends presented a problem. Since it was obvious we were not to be dissuaded, they thought we should make a record—take movies, they said. They added that we might even be able to sell the shots and pay for the film that way. "They," in this case, were professional movie makers in Hollywood; and they were persuasive, even though neither John nor I had ever taken so much as one foot of movie film. Somehow we made space in our boxes for a small 16mm camera and film—a lot of film—which cost a lot of money and really blew our budget to smithereens.

We coulda bought a boat.

Now with the canyon in total shade, waiting for John's head to appear at the top of the rapid, I tried to remember all I had been taught about taking movies. We had gotten a one-hour course on cinematography from our experts before we left, but we never had time to practice nor to see any film we had shot. The whole movie thing was a gamble. And expensive. We had actually spent more of our meager funds on the movie supplies than we had on the whole rest of the trip. Our budget for everything else was $50 each! We had though it the bargain vacation of all time—until the movie thing at least. If John came through those rapids all right and I didn't get good movies of him I was in trouble. I was almost as nervous as he was. Well . . . maybe.

Another last-minute departure from plans came through Otis Chandler, a Stanford classmate. Otis wanted to do a story on our trip for his newspaper, the *Los Angeles Times*, complete with pictures of us in our funny-looking swimming outfits. We agreed to the idea on the condition that nothing would appear in the paper until after we were in the river and couldn't be stopped. And then another friend said he wanted to do a TV interview for his station. We also agreed to that on the same condition.

In both interviews we were troubled by the questions. They

The CBS News cameraman was interested in each item of our gear.

wanted to know so many things about how we were going to accomplish our goal of swimming 280 miles of reputedly dangerous river. So many questions we really had no answers to. How could we? We had never done it before. We kept saying, "We don't know, we'll work it out." But I think it was when we were asked who our parents were and where we'd been up till now that we began to see they were thinking of what to say in our obituaries. It was during the TV interview when the guy had us out in a swimming pool in those long johns that we began to break up in giggles. After they had to take several shots over again because we weren't serious enough, the anchorman said, "You guys are supposed to be going out to die, don't make a joke of it."

So rather quickly both these attentions and our own little movie project had shoved our fun vacation out of the realm of a cheap, private little lark. The night before we left, John and I tried to foresee what it would all come to. We theorized, fantasized, guessed, reasoned and just plain wondered. Would anyone take it seriously? People already seemed to be doing just that. How dangerous would it really be? We seemed to be in a minority of two on that score. Would we really recoup all that money for camera and film? And how? Would this trip have any effect on our lives from here on out? And what effect? Who might we anger? As I have said, we both had active imaginations and there weren't many possibilities, from heroes to jerks, that we didn't speculate on.

We even wrote our wills.

The next day we departed for Lees Ferry in two cars with a friend, Dave, to help with the driving. We made three stops along the way, the first at sundown at the lower Colorado River near Needles, California, where John insisted on stopping to test the water in the river. He pronounced it cold—too cold to swim in. I responded with some reassuring words about our swimming clothes and we drove on to Pierce Ferry.

We drove at night across the Nevada desert, the last 50 miles on a dusty dirt road. Pierce Ferry turned out to be just the end of the road. We found no river, no Lake Mead, no ferry, nothing except a couple of dilapidated buildings, some gasoline drums and a pair of tents. One of the tents turned out to be full of sacks of smelly bat guano. We slept in the other.

Our first night out on our Great Adventure ended with a bang!

Before sunup the next morning we were awakened by an atomic bomb.

First the brilliant light jolted us up in our sleeping bags, then shortly after came the rumble and shaking and thunder of the blast. As quickly as we remembered we were less than 30 miles from the Nevada test site, Dave and I rolled over and went back to sleep. But John was up and off to find the Colorado River in the dawn. A couple of hours later he returned totally coated with mud.

He had found the river all right, two miles or so north, and there was still current there. He had actually taken a swim — our first in the Colorado, and reported the water mighty cold. I said of course, water was always cold at dawn. On the way back across some mud flats he had tripped. But the cold river had killed his desire for another bath; better warm and dirty than clean and cold.

Leaving my car at Pierce Ferry, the three of us drove on in John's car. That day we did a quick tour of the south rim of the Grand Canyon, acting just like any other tourists, posing for pictures, looking through the coin-operated telescopes at the little river way down there, visiting the historic Kolb brothers photographic studio to see their pictures of their 1912 run of the river. But with John covered from the neck down with mud we somehow didn't come off as your normal tourists. People stared.

We arrived at the dirt road turn off to Lees Ferry late at night, rolled out the sleeping bags on the desert and slept, or at least John did. I couldn't. The excitement and anticipation were too much. All night I thrashed around trying to imagine myself swimming through a big rapid. I only managed to frighten myself. The next morning we hustled down the road a couple of miles to Lees Ferry.

It wasn't much of a place. It was barren, with only the gauging

Bill on the brink of the Grand Canyon at Lees Ferry

station we had written to, an old stone building left over from the days of John D. Lee himself and a placid, gravelly Colorado River flowing under some low cliffs along the opposite bank. But the setting was dramatic enough. Under the rising sun were the Vermillion Cliffs, the red-banded vertical riser in one of the giant steps of the great Colorado Plateau. Out of a slit in these cliffs, finished with carving yet another of its major canyon systems, the Colorado flowed into the little sunlit valley that was Lees Ferry for a short rest before plunging down into the greatest of its works, the Grand Canyon.

As the only easy access to the Colorado River in the state of Arizona, Lees Ferry became important in Mormon leader Brigham Young's plans to expand his influence to the south and west. In 1872 he instructed John D. Lee, a faithful follower, to establish a ferry at this juncture of the Colorado and Paria rivers. Lee was a fugitive, hunted for his part in the slaughter of an entire wagon train of emigrants at the so-called Mountain Meadow Massacre in 1857. Lee established the ferry as directed by Young, but in 1877, after capture and trial, he was executed at the scene of his crime. The ferry continued to operate until 1929 when Navajo Bridge was built nearby. Lee, polygamist, murderer, and ferry boat driver, achieved immortality for his very questionable part in the building of the West.

Thanks to the 1923 U.S. Geological Survey trip which, like virtually all river trips in the Grand Canyon, started from here, all mileages downriver are measured from Lees Ferry. We carried the Survey's strip maps of the river which had all the rapids marked and enough landmarks indicated so we could measure our progress each day.

After the rush of the past several days, we didn't seem to be in a hurry that Easter Sunday morning. The sun was warm and we parked near the river while we laid out our tarps and began carefully packing our boxes, double wrapping most items in thick plastic bags just in case a box sprung a leak. We took some movies of

"Watch Out, Mister"

this, including a shot of the nearby sign which read, "No Swimming in the Colorado." John and I wrote a few postcards to friends and relatives—the only word these people ever got that we had planned to do this thing.

We put on our funny-looking swimming garb and carried the heavy boxes to the water's edge. Each of them weighed about 85 pounds. Then one of us said that we ought to have Dave shoot some film of us leaving and swimming together downstream.

More delay while the camera was broken out, set up and Dave was given his filming instructions. We would enter, swim out to midstream, drift down a way and then swim back ashore to recover the camera. By this time we were very hot in our sweatshirts, rubber shirts and long johns and the Colorado felt rather refreshing.

We swam back in to a sandbar where there were a few fishermen on a Sunday outing. When they saw us swimming ashore in our weird outfits they naturally stared, but they neither asked questions nor offered more than a nod. But while John was repacking the camera, one small boy, unfamiliar with courtesies demanded by the Code Of The West, detached himself and brazenly approached.

"You going swimming?" he asked.

"Well, yes."

"In thuh river?"

"No place else, is there?"

"Well you better watch out, mister," he said, "there's a place down there a ways where they's supposed to be some *baad* quicksand."

We promised to be careful.

2

Rapids, Icewater and Fire

We said goodbye to a solemn-looking Dave who was to take John's car back to L.A. and then waded into deep water and swam out to the main current. We were carried along surprisingly swiftly while Dave and the fishermen rapidly dwindled to small figures, Dave waving sadly and the fishermen indifferent.

The water again seemed pleasant, the canyon quiet, and John and I could talk easily to each other even when we were separated by a hundred yards or so. We didn't have much to say; we were already overwhelmed by what was happening and were each lost in our own thoughts. The small, jumbled cliffs near Lees Ferry quickly gathered themselves into steep walls which then steadily grew higher. We imagined ourselves climbing out of the canyon and looked to see how many places it seemed possible. Before too long there didn't seem to be many.

Then the quiet ended; ahead of us the river was making a

noise. We pointed nervously downstream to each other, even though we knew we hadn't gone far enough to get to the first rapid. We quickly reached the noise; the river gathered speed, there were a few ripples and waves and then it was calm again. Not a rapid, just a little riffle, but the noise was new to us.

We had gone only a couple of more miles before the vagaries of the currents separated us by a quarter of a mile or so, and swim as hard as we might, it seemed the river wouldn't let us get back together. Neither of us wanted to be that much alone, so John swam over to the narrow bank and climbed out to wait for me. After I joined him we spent a few minutes aiming John's 35mm camera at the cliffs and taking a few snapshots. When we got back into the water, we both remarked on how cold it was—much colder than it had seemed at first.

The cold water began to get downright uncomfortable as we drifted down a long corridor of cliffs. And when we rounded a slight bend and saw another long passageway with Navajo Bridge hanging high above, it became obligatory to stop again and take some movies. On our second return the water felt icy.

Drifting toward the bridge we were fascinated by its lacy arch so high above us—the last work of man we expected to see for days. Dave was supposed to be up there waiting to see us, but the bridge was so high we could barely detect whether there were any people on it, much less recognize one of them. To them we must have looked like small pieces of driftwood, if they even saw us.

Just as we passed under the bridge the canyon was rocked by an explosion that sounded like a 120mm cannon going off. Then another, and another. People were dropping small boulders off the bridge! Falling from nearly 500 feet, the boulders exploded when they hit the water. We waved frantically, but only when we were safely past the bridge did we finally see one of the little figures up in the sky seem to wave back. Must have been Dave.

The water was really beginning to seem cold now. My rubber shirt had leaked and all I could think of was getting out of that

Rapids, Icewater and Fire

water and getting warm. The Lees Ferry hydrographer notwithstanding, the actual temperature of the water that day was 51 degrees F. This is but 19 degrees above freezing and humans don't last long in water that cold.

Not only were we freezing, but we were being blinded by a wind that blasted sand and water into our eyes so that we had no recourse but to drift downstream backward. John complained bitterly that no one had mentioned the wind in the books he had read and I had to admit the same. We agreed that if it were to blow like this all the time we just might quit and go home . . . if we could.

We turned another bend and passed out of sight of the bridge and the wind blew even harder. There was nothing to do now but get out of the water and find shelter. We searched for a campsite but saw only piles of big boulders below the cliffs—not even enough room to lay out a sleeping bag. I was so cold now that I felt I would turn to stone if we didn't find a campsite soon.

Around another bend we saw a small side canyon which made a break in the cliffs on the right. Where it joined the river we saw a pile of sand and scattered boulders that had been pushed out of the side canyon during flash floods. We swam, kicking our fins with all of our strength to get to the bank before being swept past. Pushing the bulky boxes through the water and not being able to use our arms to swim made it slow going, but at the last moment the current weakened and we landed on the powdery beach just at the mouth of the little side canyon.

The wind still blew furiously as we looked for a place to build a fire and camp out of the wind. The best we could find was a little pocket among some boulders where the wind became a whirlwind blowing sand round and round with only slightly less fury than the blasts outside. When the fire got going ashes and sparks were added to the whirling sand.

When John opened up his boxes to get out his warm dry clothes, he found that water had gotten in, and while the wind and sand and ashes blew furiously outside, the Colorado River lapped calmly around his clothes and food, defying him to be comfortable. He was stunned—too miserable to rage, he could only mutter.

He rigged a clothesline and hung his clothes up, philosophically remarking that "dry and gritty is better than wet and muddy." Fortunately, most of his other things—double wrapped in plastic—were saved from the water, though he did lose some cookies and candy.

The real disaster was that the movie camera was soaked and the film loaded in it ruined! With its enormous load of silt, the river water left everything it touched gritty. And even though I stripped the camera down as much as I could—even to cleaning the shutter mechanism—it still sounded suspiciously wheezy when it ran. Another casualty was our river map. I had wrapped the first sheet in plastic and tied it to the top of one of my boxes. The plastic leaked and of course our map was a sodden mass of pulp.

It, too, was gingerly dried and though barely legible we could see that we were camped at a place called Six Mile Wash. If the river could do all that damage in only six miles, what would the next 274 miles be like? Not a comforting thought.

Finally, well after dark, we set about making dinner—no simple matter with the air full of dirt and ashes. We dined on an unpretentious canned stew flavored with cinders, sand and ashes, and washed down with strong coffee made with muddy river water. Even though we kept our pans covered between bites, whenever we lifted the lid to sneak out a forkful the wind added to the fine brown and black layer already over our meat and potatoes. It was dangerous to linger too long over a bite; in seconds the morsel would be coated. That night we found why we had brought diving masks. Wearing them around our windy campfire we could at least keep the sand and ashes out of our eyes.

Dropping off to sleep later I wondered what the rapids would be like. Would we be able to get through? Or would we be hurt—a leg broken, or a concussion? And what if we got pinned to a rock by the current? How to get free? Obviously this wasn't the first time these thoughts had surfaced, to the contrary, we had talked them to death. But now the problem was at hand.

The next morning the wind still blew, and as the sun reached over the canyon walls and forced us awake I looked over to see John with matted eyebrows, muddy face, scraggly beard, unkempt hair, face blotched with yesterday's zinc oxide ointment, all covered with a fine layer of light-colored sand and ashes. He peeked out of his sleeping bag like a dirty old caterpillar called too soon out of the cocoon. I told him he couldn't have sold life insurance to a condemned man. He in turn warned me that the first cop we saw would arrest me for vagrancy.

We were clumsy getting breakfast, having to wait for a short lull between gusts to open a box, retrieve an item and quickly close the flap before the wind blew in another cupful of sand and ashes. We fumed and muttered and the wind added sand to the flour and sand to the water and sand to the butter and sand to the syrup and our hotcakes tasted like mud pies. John still had some water in his boxes which now was mud. After breakfast we went to the river to wash dishes but in the minute it took us to walk back our dishes were dirty again. Then, as if sorry for what it had done, the wind died.

Despite the late hour, John felt an urgent need to clean all the mud out of his boxes, so he emptied them and spread all his gear out to scrape it off and let it begin to dry.

From down the canyon came a sound we had already learned. It was approaching fast. A few hundred yards away the brush bent under the approach of a tan cloud; little dust devils danced and twisted their spiral columns of sand here and there in advance of the cloud.

"Oh no!" shouted John. We both dove for his gear, scrambling and clutching, trying to stuff it willy nilly into his boxes. But too late. We were surrounded by blowing sand and there was nothing for poor John to do but sigh pitifully, turn his back to the wind and cover his eyes and nose. I did likewise. When we finally packed, it was not without a fair measure of sand in along with everything else.

We hurried into our river clothes and hustled the heavy boxes one at a time to the water's edge. Our side canyon had made a little riffle here, but the riffle was almost obliterated by the seamless texture of choppy little waves the wind made on the surface of the river. The water looked extra cold and we recalled that when we had washed dishes in it our hands had hurt from the cold. The sun was high, and though we had no watch we knew it was getting late. Even so, after looking at that forbidding water, each of us found some very necessary last minute adjustments.

John had been experimenting with a coiled lanyard and some sort of clever quick-release knot so that he could let his boxes out on a long line if he needed to. The coil was miserably snarled and needed careful attention. As soon as he finished, I realized that I had again put our mutilated map on the outside of my box; obviously that hadn't worked before, so I needed to memorize the next few miles and put it inside.

John had been waiting while I secured the map, then he saw that he ought to do a better job of sealing the waterproof flap to his boxes. After watching him take such great care, I worried that I ought to do likewise and so resealed each of mine.

Then it was the rubber shirts that needed adjustment, one after the other, then our inflatable Mae West lifejackets, and then we felt the socks we wore under our fins to prevent chafe were too full of sand so these had to be rinsed out in the muddy water. Each of these steps demanded careful discussion and experimentation.

This little one-act play in ankle-deep water must have taken about an hour, but ultimately there was nothing more we could do but get into the cold water.

It was an agony we were to feel many times a day in the weeks ahead. Wading off the silt bank into gradually deepening water, pushing our boxes ahead of us, we resisted the increasing current as long as we could, putting off the moment when we had to surrender and get swept off our feet to begin swimming toward midstream. The moment we stopped swimming we could feel our bodies try to fight off the cold. The water, of course, was relentless. Water is so much more efficient than air at conducting heat, and at little more than half the body temperature it can swiftly carry away much of whatever warmth the body is able to produce.

Our cheap little swimming outfits, rubber shirts, sweatshirts and woolen underwear helped slow down this numbing loss of heat, but only inadequately. Our bodies, to survive, had to keep our central temperature up. Faced with rapid heat loss, the body retreats, first abandoning the skin and its underlying tissues by closing off blood circulation. In arctic temperatures this can result in loss of fingers and toes to frostbite. In our cold water, frostbite was not the problem; hypothermia, or lowering of temperature of the whole body, was. The next part of our bodies to be abandoned to the cold would be our muscles and with their loss our chances of survival would diminish seriously.

We were very conscious of this from almost the first day. We could not keep warm in the river; we could not be comfortable. But to endure for the long periods we would have to stay in the water, we had to keep active. This sounds easier than it was.

On first getting into the water we felt pain everywhere on the surface of our bodies from the shock of the cold water. Soon after, especially if we stopped swimming, came a tingling, the first stage of numbness, and our reaction was to fight it, to shiver, to flex our arms, legs and feet, to swim — even to shake our heads. Soon the numbness passed, replaced by a weariness that made us think we were getting used to the cold. If we could stay in the sunlight and keep our heads dry we could forget for a while the cold creeping into our muscles from our necks down. But before long we would begin to feel stiff and resisted movement of any kind. It became easier to make no effort at all. Finally it became painful to move, we hurt all over. We became aware that something more than discomfort was happening; bones felt like icicles and wouldn't bend at the joints. We could no longer actually feel our feet, and when we struggled to limber up it hurt quite a lot. Even when we ignored the pain and forced ourselves, we could hardly move.

This was the time to get warm—the last chance. Otherwise, next would come a drowsiness from which there would be no escape; the temperature in our central organs would begin to drop and our lives would be threatened.

The noise woke me up. I was almost unaware of the last half mile, but when I heard the rumble ahead over the wind, I knew I had to act. John heard it at the same time and we both forced our nearly helpless legs to push us toward shore. We could barely see 50 yards through the blowing sand ahead but we could feel the current speeding up. At first we seemed to make no progress out of the center of the river, we were being carried against our will toward the noise. Then gradually, as before, we made more progress and the current lessened—the effort took about all the strength we had left. When we finally touched the bank we fell exhausted into the warm sand, lying there in the noise, grateful for the little bit of sun shining on us. Grateful, too, for the black rubber shirts which, if they didn't conserve our own warmth too well, certainly absorbed the sun's heat quickly.

Semi-restored, we got up and made our way down through the pile of huge boulders disgorged from the little side canyon that had split the massive cliffs. We slipped and stumbled as our paralyzed muscles refused to perform their duty. We were at Badger Creek and soon saw the source of the noise, Badger Creek Rapid. We had landed at its very head—just barely before we would have been swept down it. We found a spot alongside the midway point, sat on a boulder and soaked up more sun while we studied our first rapid.

It's not a big rapid, though to us at the time it seemed big enough. On the brink there were rocks sticking up all over the place and now and then the water swirled, revealing other rocks just under the surface. Out in the middle of the river there seemed to be a clear channel, but we saw that from where we had landed we could not swim out that far before the river carried us down the vicious edge of the rapid. The only way to get enough room to swim to midstream would be to haul our boxes well up river before launching ourselves. That didn't sound like much fun.

Another possibility was to turn our boxes loose to go through the rapid by themselves while we swam vigorously through what seemed to be the safest channel. But supposing a box or boxes were lost or pinned under a rock by the current?

We could portage, that is, carry our boxes around the rapid, but that would be more work than carrying them up river and, of course, would not be in the spirit of the whole enterprise.

We concluded that we would be best off if we tried to swim, stumble and drift along the boulder-strewn edge of the rapid. The current there seemed slower and the volume of water did not seem as if it would overpower us. Short of being pinned against a boulder or dragged over one, we should make it okay.

We guessed that it was nearly noon; anyway, we were hungry, so before returning to the icy water we dined on dried fruit and candy—quick energy but not too filling. Already we were wishing we had brought more food. Living off our rations for a few days in Los Angeles had been a good idea, but we had failed to account for the extra calories we were burning out here. And then the movie camera and film took up so much room.

Badger Creek was a fight. We writhed and squirmed and fended off rocks while our contrary boxes pulled at us or jammed in between rocks and fought our efforts to pull at them. John let out his quick-release line and at once his boxes swept around one side of a boulder while he was forced around the other side. The line naturally caught up on the rock and there was John, trapped. He couldn't pull the boxes around his way, so he had to go hand over hand up the thin nylon line against the pressure of the current to work his way around the rock. John's boxes held fast under the

Bill tricked out in full river-swimming regalia

steady pressure of the flowing water, but as soon as he got halfway around the boulder they shot downstream, jerking John off the boulder and dragging him underwater. He came up a few yards downstream, sputtering and cursing, but in the clear.

This was not the way to swim a rapid. Even at the slower rate along the edge, the current was much stronger than we were and there were just too many boulders. It was dangerous.

As we drifted below Badger Creek, we speculated that our theory of running rapids was still valid, though untested. Swimming alone we could easily avoid rocks we thought—especially if we could see them. But the problem still remained of what to do with the boxes. Without them we had all the freedom of movement we needed, but they were too bulky to shift quickly around in the water or to swim fast with. Cutting the boxes loose was simply unacceptable. We had tried to keep track of particular pieces of driftwood or logs as they went through Badger Creek Rapid and had seen how easy it was to lose sight of them. And to lose our food, clothing, matches, etc. might be really dangerous. There is not much chance of living off the land in these canyons, which were starting to get very deep.

The plateau into which the Colorado has cut its canyons rises to the west from Lees Ferry; only nine miles downstream the rim was already a thousand feet above the river, only 40 feet of that was the drop in the river bed itself. Trying to leave, to give up the attempt, was getting to look very difficult indeed. Better to stay on the river.

We were cold again, but this time we weren't going to be lulled into drifting almost to the brink of the rapid. Soap Creek Rapid made so much noise we heard it from two miles upstream. There was a booming and crashing tone to the roar which had not been there at Badger Creek. It was quite alarming. We could see the side canyon, Soap Creek Canyon, coming in from the right almost from the time we first heard its rapid, so well upstream we began to edge to the right side of the river. But soon it began to appear that we weren't going to make it: the bend in the river and the delta of Soap Creek were creating a current angle we couldn't overpower. Reversing course, we headed for the left bank, only a narrow band of boulders below the cliff, which we reached well above the beginning of the rapid. It appeared to us that at higher stages of water there would be no bank here at all, only sheer cliffs dropping straight into the river.

When we had clambered down alongside the rapid, feeling like ants on a gravel pile, it was obvious that the Badger Creek technique was out of the question. The river raged at our very feet with no appreciable slowing at its edge. It was a lot bigger rapid than Badger Creek: steeper, longer, wilder, with bigger waves and more noise. There was little likelihood we could get to the other bank without being swept over the rapid. Our only choice seemed to be to swim straight through the safest part of the rapid.

After inspecting the maelstrom from several sites, guessing at the location of a number of unseen but suspected boulders in the rapid, we concluded that a little left of center was the best course.

The place had a nasty reputation, having caused one of the early drownings—that of Frank M. Brown during an attempt to survey the Grand Canyon for a proposed railroad through it. Several of those early expeditions had dumped their boats in Soap Creek, so most had chosen to laboriously portage around. In 1929 a party of young men on a strictly-for-fun trip became its first conquerors.

Now John Daggett was about to become the first person to swim through Soap Creek Rapid. We hoped.

In addition to the camera and tripod, I had brought my fins and life jacket from upstream. From where I stood, well below the brink of the rapid, it would not be hard to scramble downstream and launch myself into the river below the rapid if John needed help.

What did John think about as he was stumbling back upstream to get ready to swim the rapid? Mostly, he said, that he didn't want to get back into that cold water. Regardless of what other dangers the river might offer, as far as John was concerned the most immediate was its temperature. He had no fear of death. Since the loss of his wife and two little girls less than a year previously, it was something that really didn't matter much. He was somewhat afraid of being seriously injured — especially with no help available except old Bill sitting down there on his rock.

He put on his fins and life jacket rather quickly and, with a deep breath, shoved off into the river.

He found himself lying face down between his two boxes, which were loosely joined by their straps, with one arm draped over each. He could hoist his head a foot or so off the water to better see where he was going and he had his legs free for kicking.

Down on my rock I was busy practicing with the camera, following chunks of driftwood as they slid down the long smooth tongue of the rapid and were lost in the boiling waves and confusion below. It was hard to follow them — about the best I could do was hope to pan the camera with the flow of the water so that when the chunk of driftwood did surface it was still in the frame.

Then I saw John at the top of the rapid waving. I checked that the camera was wound and aimed it at him. Through the viewfinder, like looking through the wrong end of a telescope, I saw only a wall of water with a tiny figure perched on top. The little figure swooped down the smooth wall and was immediately lost in the angry, noisy water. I could feel the camera grinding the film as I tried to follow the path through the water I thought John would travel. But where was he?

Suddenly he popped to the top of a wave, very close, almost filling the viewfinder. I could see his expression. Pain? No, more like intent. Then he dropped down behind a wave. Just as he came out on the other side of it, another wave reached over and smacked him on the side of the head and he disappeared again. Then almost as fast as he had disappeared, he reappeared. He was only a spit away from me and I could have jumped in next to him. The camera stopped and I had to rewind it.

I was diverted for only a moment, but when my attention turned back to John he was 50 yards downstream and waving to me that everything was all right. I could see him shouting something, but couldn't hear over the noise of the rapid. I kept the camera pointed at him, filming until he faded away into the gloom that now filled the canyon.

Drifting in the shadows below Soap Creek Rapid, John was relaxed and elated. He had had a whale of a good time going through that rapid, but now that the excitement had passed, he realized that he had been very tense during his ride. He wondered why; there wasn't anything to it—he had seen and swum in much more dangerous waters in Pacific breakers. He thought of me and wished he could have told me what fun it was. He realized that though I would be a bit worried, I'd have no trouble. So he turned his thoughts to finding a good place to camp and getting a warm fire going.

Back at Soap Creek I was all alone. And believe me, there's no place lonelier. John was out of sight around a bend and what I had to do I had to do all by myself—nobody to even watch. I gathered up the camera, tripod, fins and lifejacket and went back upstream to my boxes. I wasn't as frightened now—after all, John had gotten through all right—all I had to do was jump in and swim the rapid and get downstream to where John had started camp. I packed the camera, sealed the box and got in the water.

It was late afternoon and the water was really cold! I kicked hard to get out in the middle and got there sooner than needed. So there was nothing to do for a few moments except drift toward the noise of the unseen rapid. I hung suspended in the smooth water not moving. Little pieces of driftwood hovered a few inches away barely cracking the glassy surface. Nothing moved. And yet everything was moving rapidly toward the brink. I could hear the noise and beyond the brink I could see plumes of the waves leaping up here and there. But of the rapid itself I could see nothing.

Then in a moment I was on the brink. With no time to think I dropped swiftly down the fast, smooth, undulating slide into the waves and fury. I was immediately pulled under, or maybe through, the first wave. I came up and the spray smashed into my face so that I couldn't see a thing. I went under again, came up, got twisted around and was bounced up and down like a ping pong ball on a water fountain. The waves were so powerful I could hardly keep my feet under me. I was hanging onto my boxes with all my strength while the river pulled at me from all directions. It even tried to pull the swim fins off my feet. I was a little alarmed at my helplessness.

Almost instantly I was in control again in the choppy tail of the rapid that streamed down the river for a quarter of a mile. Now I could see what was happening to me.

It had been a wild ride but a lot of fun. I lost a lot of fear of rapids there and then—in fact, I looked forward to the next one. This was a great sport! It reminded me of the first thrill of skiing or riding a breaking wave. The only thing wrong was that it was so cold.

In all the violence, water had leaked in again under my rubber shirt and my sweatshirt was drawing in cold water like a wick, making me ever colder. And I was lonely. The canyon wasn't awesome and beautiful anymore—just gloomy. I wanted to rejoin John and sit by a warm fire and gloat about swimming our first big rapid. I began to search the darkening shore for smoke or flame or John. Perhaps he was up around the next bend.

As I came around slowly I searched every inch of shore. A small rapid chattered away and I ran it without hesitation. Of course I got my face and head wet again and was colder still. Now it was my teeth that chattered. There was another bend around to the left, and as I came around I was facing a straight calm stretch of water almost two miles long. Here and there were piles of boulders that had fallen from the vertical cliffs and I knew that in one of them John was right now setting up camp. I drifted along colder and stiffer by the minute, occasionally yelling so I wouldn't drift by without his noticing. He might be busy behind a rock where I had no chance of seeing him. The wind was still blowing hard and he would naturally seek a very protected site. With the long run it had in this straight corridor, the wind whipped up bits of spray and sand and blew this mixture into my eyes making it hard to see.

Then I heard another rapid. It had a deep sound—probably not a small rapid. Of course John would camp above it. As I approached the rapid I looked for the side canyon which had formed it. Everything was shadowy and I couldn't see it, so not knowing which bank the side canyon delta and John would be on, I stayed in the middle of the river. As I got closer I saw that there wasn't any side canyon! The cliffs were unbroken above and below the rapid on both sides. This turned out to be Sheer Wall Rapid, so named because it had been formed by chunks of cliffs falling off on both sides. I could land and scout it but had better hurry up.

To hell with it! I was so helpless with cold that I didn't even want to get out of the water to look over a rapid. If I got out, I wouldn't have been able to get back in again. All I wanted to do was get to a fire. After all, John must have run the thing. Or at least he had if I hadn't already passed him. So down I went.

I was too cold to really appreciate it at the time, but it was fun. It had a ten-foot drop and some nice big bouncy waves. Just beyond the rapid there was yet another big bend, and as I glided around I saw another straight stretch of more than a mile. And still no John.

Where was he? Didn't he know I was freezing? Wind rushing up the canyon smacked me in the face and I swore. I was not only cold, now I was getting angry. John wasn't showing any sense getting so far ahead; he should have waited in shallow water or on a mud bank. But maybe he wasn't ahead? Maybe I had passed him

Rapids, Icewater and Fire

near one of the rapids where I was too blinded or too busy to look? Now I didn't know whether to go on to catch up or stop to wait. What if I did stop and he never showed up? Then he would be as baffled as I, not knowing whether I had passed him or stopped short. His best guess would have to be that I had gotten in trouble and was still upstream of him. Then of course he'd have to try the nearly impossible—go up the Colorado. In that event, if I'd already passed him, he would be struggling futilely.

We each had a pistol for signaling in an emergency, but with all the cliffs and echoes such signals would probably be only confusing.

I was really cold by now, desperately so. I had to stop soon simply to survive. I had already traveled four miles downstream from Soap Creek and had been in the water for what seemed like half a day, though it was more like an hour. It was virtually dark, so I resolved to go around the next bend and, if I couldn't see John, to stop anyway and set up my own camp. I was rather glad now we had packed for self sufficiency.

Just at the head of that next bend was another small rapid. I stayed in the center of the river, playing it safe. Then miraculously, there was John over on the left bank just above the rapid waving frantically.

Too late.

I tried to swim over to him. I wanted so much to get out of the water immediately. But the river as always had too much strength. I was dragged over the little rapid, not in the nice deep water but along the shallow edge, bouncing and swearing and barking my shins and thumping my ankles until I finally made a landing just below the rapid. Then I had a long, muddy 75 yards to carry my heavy boxes, one at a time. By the time I made camp I was the wettest, coldest, maddest, tiredest, stiffest, sorest man in Arizona.

I barely had strength to plop down in the lee of the boulders in the little sandy spot John had picked for camp and start giving him hell. But I couldn't get too angry, after all, we were back together again with good reason to celebrate the afternoon, and John did have a satisfactory explanation for going so far. He had been particularly anxious to find a spot out of the wind after last night, and had even gotten out of the water once or twice at likely spots, but none had satisfied him so he had gone on. As a matter of fact, he had arrived at our camp just a few minutes before I came around the bend and hadn't even started the fire.

I never knew what a blessing to mankind fire was till at last we got our bit of flame going. I didn't care if I never moved away from the fire—I was so exhausted that I had no appetite and only wanted to crawl in a warm sleeping bag and sleep. It had been a day of doubts and fears, triumphs, tribulations and exhilarations that neither of us would forget for the rest of our lives. For the moment, contemplation had to take a back seat while we enjoyed the miraculous restorative powers of the hot chicken soup John served up.

3

Getting in Deeper

The next morning we were filled with optimism. We enthused about our successes at Soap Creek, Sheer Wall and the other small rapids we had run in those last long hours of the day before. Rapids swimming was fun! We looked forward to the 160 or so ahead of us with a forgivable, if perhaps premature, overconfidence.

"If Soap Creek is supposed to be so tough, I don't think this river is all it's cracked up to be. In fact, it's a cinch."

"Yes, but what if there had been a sharp rock or two right in the middle, just under the surface?"

That threat was waved off as merely hypothetical—our real problem was time. We were behind the daily mileage we had planned to swim and earnestly hoped for more rapids to speed us up.

We examined the map closely and guessed that we had landed at Mile 16½.

"So today we get an early start and swim till late—maybe we can make 20 miles or more."

But our resolutions notwithstanding, we still took about 45 minutes after breakfast to pack and get dressed. By the time were were ready the sun was already over the canyon rim and shining on the water.

We eased ourselves into the frigid water, were snatched up by the river and were immediately on our way. We hardly had time to look back at our little camp before we were swept through the small rapid I had run the night before, then around the bend and into House Rock Rapid. It had a nice, easy, ten-foot drop, and we felt a little rush of excitement in the fast water and waves and then we were in calm water.

We were carried along another mile or so while the walls slowly closed in, until the river lapped up against the foot of the cliffs leaving no bank, not even a pile of boulders. There would be no getting out of the river here. And then around the next bend we saw, right in the middle of the river, what appeared to be a house. No, it was a boulder! What an explosion that thing must have made when it fell off the cliff. On the side of the boulder we chose, the river narrowed down to about 30 feet; the other side was even narrower. In flood the rock would be covered.

We saw a little beach ahead near 19 Mile Canyon and pulled over to take photos of this spot and also to warm up as we were both extremely cold already. After landing and taking a few shots, lunch seemed like a good idea. We carried our lunches in plastic and rubber bags tied to our life jackets, and did the same with one of our still cameras; eating and photographing were two frequent activities during the day for which we didn't want to have to unbuckle and unseal our intricate rubber boxes. Taking movies would be more of an operation than just snapping the shutter, so the movie camera and film remained sealed in their respective boxes most of the time.

After lunch we again eased into the cold water, screeching and

Getting in Deeper

howling to the canyon walls as the agony crept higher and higher on our briefly warmed bodies. Somehow or other it helped to yell and holler whenever we got into the water.

The next rapid was only a mile or so down river. We could hear it growling loudly so we decided to look it over. We landed just above North Canyon and worked our way over the warm sand and boulders to the foot of the rapid. It did look a little rough with a 15-foot drop in about the first 50 feet of the rapid.

Below the rapid was a huge eddy that caught our attention. An area the size of a city lot was solid with driftwood slowly wheeling around with the upstream edge reaching almost to the head of the rapid. In the middle of this desert Sargasso Sea was a large log; it looked like a telephone pole. For a half hour or so John and I tried in vain to push the log out of the eddy into the current, but the big whirlpool was too strong. Even the couple of times we seemed to get it halfway out into the main stream, the whirlpool always reclaimed it. Pretty soon we stopped playing.

"Hey, we've run worse rapids than this."

"Yeah, we can't waste any more time."

So we went back to our boxes and into the water again. We went down over North Canyon Rapid with a sudden rush that made me think of that first long swoop on a roller coaster when you shoot to the bottom then back up again and you have that funny tingling in your stomach. Only in a rapid it's different. You can't always see and there is lots of water and noise and it's all very confusing what with going sideways and sometimes getting turned around backwards or even being flipped end for end.

We were no sooner out of North Canyon Rapid than we were in 21 Mile Rapid and then another one, where we were both scared out of our wits when we blindly ran into each other. We were still untangling when we shot into another rapid and then still another.

What a ride! We had run almost three miles of nearly continuous rapids with scarcely a minute to breathe. In that distance the river had dropped 40 feet. We both thought it was hilarious fun and wished that the whole rest of the river could be like that.

But then we had a calm stretch. There weren't any rapids, though the river moved along swiftly, faster than we were used to in previous calm stretches. This cheered us up and we were sure that we were making that 20 miles we had targeted. But calm water meant cold. We weren't so active so we had time to think about the cold. My rubber shirt was leaking and I was even colder than John. I wanted to stop. But at my hollered insistence that we stop and warm up, John shouted back that we ought to keep going. Not wanting to separate, we agreed that we would run one more rapid and then stop.

We had scarcely had time to look at the walls of the canyon for the last few miles, but with a few minutes of quiet before the next rapid we noticed our imprisoning walls had already risen to nearly three thousand feet. We could seldom see the desert plateau because the lower set of cliffs rising from near the water's edge, like the walls of some giant castle, blocked our view. This is the Red Wall Limestone, the Grand Canyon's most massive formation, the formation which gave the name to Marble Canyon. Its sheer, regularly cracked mass makes it look like a wall of perfectly fitted, unmortared, huge stone blocks. It is painted dull red with vertical orange and brown streaks, hundreds of feet long, tapering down from its brink. This red paint job came from an eroding shale above. At the water's edge, though, the stone is a mottled gray, like most limestones, with here and there a streak of yellow or green or purple. This great homogeneous slab of marble encircles the canyons from one to two thousand feet below the rim—the most spectacular of all the formations. It is also the one most responsible for the inaccessibility of the bottom as its vertical walls are only broken where a side canyon has cut a narrow staircase.

The upper set of cliffs loomed above the Red Wall—another giant step to the sky. We could see these only at the ends of the straight stretches of the canyons because when the Red Wall was near it blocked out everything but a small strip of sky. The immen-

Sheer cliffs and blowing silt at Marble Canyon

sity of our surrounding world constantly impressed us. Quiet contemplation was one of our more pleasant diversions.

But never for long. At that moment 24 Mile Rapid growled at us with its promise of danger, fun and, best of all, warmth on the dry bank beyond. As soon as I passed through the noisy bouncing world of spray and waves, I pulled immediately for shore.

The first thing I did was pull the bottom of my rubber shirt away from my skin, and as I did so, about three quarts of Colorado River poured out. No wonder I was cold; about the only value of the rubber shirt was that it had slightly slowed down the circulation of the water.

Something prompted me to unbuckle one of my rubber boxes to take out my camera. When I did I found my enthusiasm for this day draining away. My "waterproof" box had leaked and my poor little camera was dripping wet. The shutter seemed sticky; it would only work at speeds between $1/25$ and $1/100$, and there was no way of telling whether it was actually shooting at those speeds. On top of that, an entire roll of film had been ruined.

I wanted to stop here and dry out my camera, saying to John there wasn't much point in going on if I couldn't take pictures. It had turned into a nice calm sunny afternoon with no blowing sand, perfect for the job. The thought of getting back into the cold water was as discouraging as the wet camera.

So I took my little 35mm camera apart, and put the pieces on a rock in the sun, and volunteered to have a look at the movie camera. John dug into his box only to find, when he unwrapped the movie camera, that it, too, had gotten wet again. Well, that precipitated a nice little discussion , after which John, stung by my criticisms, went off in a huff to try some target practice with his pistol.

I took up my hunting knife and pliers and attacked the movie camera. I got the cover off, shearing only one tiny screw; then as I was probing into the mechanism for the next step, the ever-poised little spring flew out and whinged off into the sand somewhere. Immediately all the tiny parts of the shutter mechanism fell into a heap in my palm. I was very glad John wasn't watching.

Getting in Deeper

The real miracle was finding that little spring, half buried in the sand ten feet away. After that, solving the Chinese puzzle of parts was easy. After an hour or so the shutter ran, sounded healthy and looked right. There was, however, some doubt as to whether the opening was in proper phase with the film movement. There were twelve possible positions and only one would work.

As I put the clean, dry, smooth sounding camera away I fought off a nagging feeling that something wasn't quite right. Then I remembered a spot of rust on the shutter that had been visible in the lens socket. I unscrewed the lens and saw no rust spot. Had I cleaned it off? Or was it still there hidden behind the cover? On such things hang important matters. Film or no film might make a major difference in our project. Things were not going right.

So off came the front of the camera and lo, there was my little rust spot, the size of a pin head, taunting me. I shifted the shutter, but was now really uncertain just where it should be mounted. Should I rely on a hazy memory and a defiant little rust spot? I was afraid to tell John, but I would wonder whenever we shot movies whether the time and effort were producing anything.

John, in the meantime, was banging away at a tin can, whooping and praising himself whenever he hit it and watching the bullet hit the sand when he missed. Then one shot neither hit the can nor the sand. Most people would have assumed they hadn't seen the miss and shot again, but John's old Marine habits caused him to automatically look in the barrel. Sure enough, there was the bullet, stuck. The next shot might have blown his hand off, or worse.

Together we struggled to drive the bullet out of the barrel, succeeding only after I had taken a good gouge out of my hand. It was not my day.

John next decided, of all things, to take a swim. Stripped to the buff with an amused and curious Bill following him, he went to the water's edge. John never hesitates about going into the water, so after quickly estimating the depth, he plunged in. He was beneath the muddy surface for only a second. Then he shot halfway out of the water, let out a huge scream and raced for shore.

"What happened, John?"

"Oooh, Wow! Oooh, my God! That water is COLD!"

"That's a funny thing to say after swimming 20 odd miles in it."

"Yeah, but I didn't think it was *that* cold. I sure appreciate those rubber shirts and long johns now. You should try it — go ahead."

"No thanks," I said.

We were a little lost that night. It seemed to us that we must have traveled to about Mile 29, but we had not seen any unmistakable landmarks noted on our strip maps, which only showed the river's edges. Later we were able to deduce that we had in fact camped at 24 Mile Rapid. It was a problem which would plague us from time to time, and we began to learn that night to carefully observe and remember landmarks. Not that we could get lost but it was important to know how far we had gone and what lay just ahead.

Our third night in the canyons and already we had a comfortable routine. While I started the fire, John dug out the canvas bucket and filled it with water to let the silt settle. Otherwise the Colorado River water, which had been described as, "too thick to drink and too thin to plow," was pretty gritty to drink or use in mixes. Firewood was easy; the river always carried with it tons and tons of driftwood, which it smashed into kindling and logs. In flood season the river deposited this supply here and there high on its banks where it baked in the desert sun. One match usually lighted it easily.

After dinner, which we cooked separately — often competing to see whose dinner could elicit the most envy — came the quiet hour when we sipped coffee or whatever, and each wrote in our diaries. It was a time of agreed and enforced silence. It was also when I missed smoking most. I had given it up for the trip — partly because of the lack of space caused by all that movie film. Some way to give up smoking.

Getting in Deeper

On this night the wind had died down and we could look up at the brilliant strip of stars between the canyon walls. With no city lights for hundreds of miles, we could see stars we'd never seen. The only thing to tell us we weren't on another planet were the occasional airplanes that flew soundlessly, high overhead, moving pinpoints of light among the stars.

We were both sore and stiff all over. Using muscles we seldom used had given us each a collection of knots. We were sunburned, and our feet were sore and tender from walking barefooted on sharp, hot rocks and from the constant chafing of the fins. Our hands were particularly chapped and sore from being soaked in cold water and dried in hot sun again and again each day. Windburn and a collection of cuts and abrasions in various places completed the toll.

Wednesday, April 13, was our fourth day on the river and we were feeling like pros. We were smooth and efficient that morning and were in the river as soon as there was sunlight shining on it — we could have been earlier, but that muddy water in early morning shadow was too forbidding. Nankoweap Creek was our goal for the day. We hoped to camp there and spend part of the next day exploring the cliff dwellings nearby and shooting some scenes for our movie.

We didn't make Nankoweap until two days later.

Our first rapid of the day was only a few hundred yards below our camp. As I shot down its short tongue I could see I had made a mistake. Right in front of me, too late to avoid, was a big hump, which meant a submerged boulder. Just behind it was a deep hole with the characteristic wave on its downstream side, constantly curling upstream as if to try to fill the hole. On both sides of the hole the river level was more or less normal. In the ocean, waves move toward shore, but in the river the water moves and the wave stays in one place continually breaking and reforming.

I was lying between my boxes and just had time to pull them together under my chest when I hit the rock. It knocked the wind out of me and rapped my knees hard as I slithered over it head first into the hole. The wave caught me and threw me up and back down into the hole again. I was rolled over several times, feeling like a pebble in a cement mixer before I was able to kick free. Nasty thing.

The next rapid followed quickly and sounded noisy so we stopped and gave it a look. Good thing, too, for there, right in the channel we'd have chosen, lurked a mean-looking, sharp rock poised like a knife point just at the surface. It could have easily gutted one of us.

We quickly agreed on the best side to pass the rock and returned to the water. We ran the rapid in a mad rush and went swirling downstream around a bend and smack into another rapid for the longest ride yet. There were really several rapids strung together with a total length of over a mile. We blasted into this wild, roaring stretch, bouncing down it, hollering with joy at the speed and power of the mighty river that was sweeping us along, tearing down gigantic cliffs, gouging out the trench of the canyon, but was unable to hurt us little bits of jetsam hitching a ride on its crest.

Then we sighted a cave in the cliffs and I recalled a place on the map named Cave Springs Rapid. But that was at Mile 25.5 and we were sure we had already gone farther than that last night. There wasn't much time to speculate because suddenly we were in another rapid—and right after that, another one, and yet another. No time for navigation, but now doubt lingered. If that had really been Cave Springs Rapid we were a good deal farther behind than we thought.

For the next few miles the rapids were farther apart, though as soon as we were out of one we could hear the next. Probably because the cliffs here were so smooth and unbroken they reflected sound well. We were so low in the water that we couldn't see a rapid until we were just on the brink—so we used the shape and direction of the strip of sky above to tell us what the river would likely be below. And we studied the side canyons to learn something of the rapids they formed. Obviously, we couldn't take the time to get out and survey each rapid, so we generally kept to the middle of the river and just plowed through. Each rapid added something to our knowledge and skill, and in the calm spots we compared notes.

The first man on the brink would always signal to the one behind his estimation of the best place to enter. Then if a mistake was made, perhaps only one would make it. We had learned back at 21 Mile Rapid not to stay too close—we wanted no more collisions. At the same time, we didn't want to get too far apart—Soap Creek Rapid had taught that. We were particularly careful to watch each other at a rapid to see that each got through safely. Going through, however, it was every man for himself and hang on tight. So far neither of us had been hurt badly, though we had each had several minor collisions with rocks.

A rapid is like the spillway of a dam. Something, generally a side canyon, pushes big boulders out into the main stream, narrowing it and backing up the water, sometimes for as much as two or three miles. The river gathers itself behind the rapid and then with a great roar and terrible force rushes over the boulders. As it gathers speed it forms a long smooth, gradually narrowing slope called a tongue. This smooth tongue is spotted here and there with humps which usually mark boulders close to the surface. There is seldom any danger in the tongue, but as you travel down it, the waves and rocks seem to close in from the sides and suddenly there you are in all the spray and confusion and noise. Here is where the big holes and curling waves lurk, along with their concealed or partly concealed rocks.

As the river streams out below the rapid the waves form a tapering tail. On either side of this fast water lurk scores of whirlpools or eddies. Of varying sizes and speeds, some of them are no more than a few feet across with a little sucking vortex that makes a hole five or six inches deep in the water and could spin us around like a top, even ducking us underwater occasionally; while others are huge masses of slowly swirling water covering nearly an acre and usually filled with driftwood from edge to edge. But of whatever size, we were learning to hate them with a passion.

Once through the main part of a rapid, we fought to stay in the diminishing tail—that was the only way downstream. If we got shoved out we found ourselves in a whirlpool being dragged unwillingly back upstream. It was frustrating in the extreme to be going upstream while your friend bounced happily by you going the other way. Usually there was nothing we could do but wait till the whirlpool took us up to the beginning of the tail where we could hope to swim out of its grip and start the contest all over again. Sometimes we would get out of one whirlpool and back into the current only to bounce along a few yards and get pulled out by a whirlpool on the other side. Little wonder then that after safely shooting a fast rapid and happy to be rocketing along, we ranted and raved when one of those things grabbed us. Boats, even oar-powered ones, have sufficient strength to pay these obstacles little mind, but we overburdened swimmers had very little power in that river.

We were now in a stretch where the walls were very close to us—they often rose straight up from the water leaving no bank, not even a stray boulder, to climb out on. And when the river went around a bend and the main current shifted over to one side we would find ourselves cruising along only two or three feet from the base of the sheer cliffs. Then new formations began to rise out of the water which were not homogenous like the limestone of the Red Wall but layered. They came up rapidly, sometimes a new one appeared every 50 feet or so. As they rose higher we began to see that they were not going to remain a solid wall. They seemed to be more susceptible to erosion; the river was cutting into some of them making ledges and overhangs. These made us nervous as we weren't anxious to get swept in under a rock overhang. We kept more to the middle of the river.

A new diversion in this stretch was the echoes. Yelling at the top of our voices, we could pile echo upon echo as the sound

Getting in Deeper

bounced back and forth between the smooth, hard, vertical walls so close alongside. It was fun until John began calling out the name of one of his dead little girls and the canyons reverberated with her name. I caught a convenient whirlpool and let John get out of range.

The next rapid was welcome, its booming sound dominated the canyon. When I came to the top and looked down I saw a tiny figure at the foot of the rapid going nowhere. John, caught in another whirlpool. As I passed him riding swiftly along in the tail I could hear him faintly over the roar of the water, cursing and panting and bewailing his luck.

The next rapid was a mile away and just beyond it the canyon took a sharp turn to the east. I was sure it would be Vasey's Paradise and yelled back at John that I would stop there. I wasn't positive we had gotten that far, but I was positive I was darn cold again, partly due to another leak in my rubber shirt. Those things were supposed to seal at our waists and arms, but movement always broke the seals — especially at the waist. And in rapids we did move a lot sometimes. At the tail of the next rapid I pulled out early, caught the whirlpool and was gently carried over to the shore and into knee deep water. John followed quickly and we climbed on shore. It had been an excellent morning, but we were both so cold that standing in the sun wasn't enough. Since we were standing near a very large pile of driftwood, the logical connection suggested itself.

The pile was five or six feet high and covered a quarter of an acre, so pretty soon we had quite a blazing bonfire. We had to stand 30 yards away, each on his own boulder turning round and round in a sort of Grand Canyon Get Warm Dance.

John was warm in more ways than one. When he opened up his little plastic lunch bag he found that the river had gotten in and his food was all soggy. He complained bitterly, "What do I have to do? I wrapped my lunch in three bags and still this damn river works its way in. You can't keep your food dry, the best you can do is cut the circulation of water down so it won't wash away."

I chuckled at poor John's misfortune. Until I found my lunch was soaked too. Then John got curious as to how his camera had fared. He had it in its own "waterproof" bag, but he hadn't gotten this bag opened yet when he declared, "Bill, I think I hear water sloshing around in there." And sure enough, he pulled out a dripping camera. When he opened it up water poured out from inside. A fine situation! Our fourth day on the river and so far every picture we had taken had been ruined.

And we still weren't sure how far we had come in those four days—we really needed the confirmation of Vasey's Paradise, which we were sure had to be close by. So this time ignoring our camera and lunch problem, we returned to the water. Another mile of calm water, then a small rapid and the river bent to the left. This time the bend kept on going, nearly doubling back on itself, and as it did so there unfolded before us one of the most spectacular things in this land of the spectacular. Here, where one marvel can only be compared to another marvel, Vasey's Paradise is outstanding.

The Red Wall is so sheer as to appear almost polished. It swoops up from the river for hundreds of feet and from each side seems to reach out over the river. Cascading down this wall are red and brown streaks, painted stalagtites put there by the thunderstorms of the past hundred centuries or so. On the right bank the cliffs are alive with springs—little freshets of clear water that pour out of the solid rock itself. As they trickle down to the Colorado they paint green stalagmites of mosses, ferns and other plants on the red cliffs.

The Paradise, however, presented us with a new problem which prevented much sightseeing. There in the middle of the river was a confusing collection of gravel bars and islands through, over and around which the river flowed. We hadn't dealt with fast-moving water flowing over shallows. I chose to keep to the right in hopes of staying in deep water, but quickly saw I had erred. Before me was an island, wide and low, which promised a bumpy ride. So

Getting in Deeper

I signaled to John to keep left. He did so and immediately found himself in a mess.

The main current was indeed on the left side, but the water there was just as shallow, merely faster. John was dragged over the rocks like a button flushed down a washboard. He tried to manipulate his fancy release knot to reduce his draft; naturally it fouled and he was soon thoroughly bound with 75 feet of parachute cord. He was tumbled down the wash end for end in a snarled mass of legs, arms, boxes, head, and nylon line, struggling to get a breath of air, trying to fend off the staccato hammering of the rocks that seemed to come from every direction, pounding him black and blue from scalp to soles. He got turned around and his back was slammed into a protruding boulder, the current pinning him for a moment of pain, then jerking him off when his boxes yanked on his nylon line and dragged him into deeper water. While he untangled himself, he looked for me.

There I was, a quarter mile upstream, standing up in the middle of the river. I had gotten by one island but had been swept up onto the second. There was nothing to do but portage my boxes over to the channel where John had seen so much trouble. The current was swift and, though the water was seldom even thigh deep, it was impossible to stand. Almost unintentionally I propped myself between my boxes, face up, and stuck my feet out pointing downstream. I could see what was ahead and was able to fend off with my feet, skipping from rock to rock occasionally bouncing my bum on the river bed, but not taking the terrible pounding John had. Thus we learned another trick in our growing knowledge of how to swim rapids. We were to use this technique more than once in the weeks ahead.

One of our main concerns before we even saw the Colorado River was what to do with our boxes. They were heavy and solid and we initially envisioned them as a liability in a rapid. After all, no one wants to be repeatedly hammered by a solid 85-pound block, even if it *is* sheathed in rubber. Two of them at once would be impossible to fend off. Furthermore, we felt that we would be better at swimming in boulder strewn rapids if we were unencumbered. Therefore, we considered that it might be best to separate ourselves from our boxes in a rapids—but since we didn't want to lose them completely, we thought of a long lanyard tying them to us. These ideas were largely discarded in the first few days on the river. We began to stay with our boxes in all the rapids, even the largest.

We had evolved two other basic ways to turn our boxes from liabilities into assets. Since they had flat, hard bottoms with straps attached, we joined these together so that we had, in effect, a sling between the boxes. In calm water we could sit on this sling, lifting our heads and shoulders out of the water—a great help in keeping warm and providing more visibility. However, in this position we had little swimming power, so when we were about to enter a rapid or wanted to escape a whirlpool we had to turn over and lie on the sling, one box under each shoulder. In this position we had more swimming power and it was easy to twist so that the boxes served as buffers to protect us in any collision with rocks.

Below Vasey's Paradise the river again turns to the southwest, and in the center of the turn is one of the canyon's most notable features, Red Wall Cavern, a huge amphitheater cut into the Red Wall at the water's edge. It looked nearly big enough for a regulation football field. But before we could pull over the current swept us past. Not far below the cavern we saw some other caves with cryptic numbers painted on the cliffs nearby. We pulled over to have a look and realized we were seeing, not natural caves, but borings for a proposed dam. We were saddened to think someone might consider submerging Vasey's Paradise and Red Wall Cavern along with most of the rest of the Marble Gorge.*

---

*After a long, bitter, very close nationwide battle, this purely hydroelectric dam and another which would have flooded most of the Grand Canyon were finally killed by Congress in 1968. By that time, Glen Canyon Dam was built and beautiful Glen Canyon already destroyed.

Climbing up to these shafts, we began to notice that going barefoot on the rasp-like sandstone rocks was becoming painful. So much so that the cold Colorado was soothing to our feet when we returned.

The shadows had begun to stretch all the way across the river and our first day of fairly pleasant weather was coming to an end. As if to underscore that fact, the wind began again, but this time it was a hot desert wind and made us feel a bit like we were up to our chests in ice water in front of a furnace flue. Then John said, "Hey Bill, I think one of my boxes is sinking. Does one look lower to you?" Sure enough, he had a list, so we started looking for a campsite. But the vertical walls of the canyon and the steep talus slopes provide few campsites along this stretch, so we drifted along for several miles, running only one rapid before finding a most dramatic place to camp.

We stopped on a little beach at the mouth of a remarkable niche in the canyon wall. Geologists call it a hanging valley, but it was much more than that. A V-shaped wedge had been cut down from the lip of the cliffs through which a sliver of pale blue sky widened our narrow horizon only slightly. Below this wedge a giant alcove had been cut back into the cliff, and below that a second one only slightly smaller. Either one would have held the stage and proscenium of a major concert hall. And below them was yet a third alcove connected to the river by a narrow defile through which we could work our way up inside. Walking up this tiny canyon we saw the rocks were covered with a thin lime coating as though they had been whitewashed. It was the same lime that streaked down the lip of each alcove. Once inside the canyon we found the floor covered with green ferns and grasses fed by a little spring seeping out of the base of the Red Wall. We had found a paradise to equal Vasey's.

We camped just at the mouth of the tiny canyon where there was shelter from the wind and clear water nearby. Then John, not without apprehension, opened his boxes.

Pandora's shock couldn't have been worse. Not one, but both his boxes had leaked—nay the river had poured in—and everything in his world was again soaking: food, clothing, sleeping bag, camera, the works. Nearby was a pile of driftwood with two or three cords of good dry wood in it, which he lit. As the wood began to blaze we dragged all John's gear over to it and, with a couple of tree limbs turned into drying racks, pretty soon we had the Grand Canyon looking like washday in Brooklyn.

During dinner, at what was becoming our nightly summing up, our map study showed us to be camped just beyond Mile 38. We had made 14 miles that day, dropping 105 feet—half of that in the first four miles. No wonder we had such a mad wild ride that morning. But 38 miles in three and a half days put us one full day behind schedule—we were moving at three-quarter speed.

And the river was taking its toll. Ruined food, wet gear, torn clothes, lost film, and damaged cameras could be just the beginning. Both of us were sore and stiff to the point of being in pain—John particularly had taken some hard raps at Vasey's Paradise today. Our faces and hands were becoming badly chapped and our hands and feet were a mass of small cuts and scrapes. My rubber shirt had a bad tear which our patching kit wouldn't fix. It seemed as if we were beginning to be worn down by bits and pieces in the same way the Colorado had carved out its mighty canyons.

On the positive side, we had swum some 25 or so rapids successfully and were getting more adept with each new one. We had devised effective techniques for each problem we faced from swimming in the rapids to camping in the canyon. Some of our pains were just preliminaries to getting in top physical condition and would likely disappear soon.

But best of all, we were having fun.

4

Blood and Fear

The next morning we again set as our goal Nankoweap Rapid, 11 miles downstream, where we wanted to explore and film at the official start of the Grand Canyon.

We didn't make it by a damsite . . . a dead river runner . . . and a dead President.

We were late getting off that day—we guessed about 11 o'clock—partly because most of John's gear was still wet and muddy and he futzed with it a lot trying to get it clean and packed. And then after a mile and a half of calm river we pulled over to look at some more damsite exploration shafts, scrambling barefoot over the hot, sharp boulders to get up to them. One had a spring of clear water trickling out; the water tasted good. Then we got back in the river, only to get out again in another hundred yards or so when we spotted some large bridge pontoons.

There were five of them, partially embedded in silt near the edge of the river. As we were wondering how they got here we saw a long cable coming down from the rim, 3,000 feet above us. The cable terminated at a little shack hanging on the lip of the Red Wall about one thousand feet above us.*

John wanted to get one of the pontoons afloat and insisted on digging away at the silt with bare hands while I argued that it was a waste of effort, wouldn't float anyway, and we were already pretty late today. An hour or so later I won and we dipped into the icy water once again. Now we knew we had some cold and miserable hours ahead to make up for our dawdling at the damsite.

Around the next bend we came upon a new landmark, Royal Arches. Were the arches in any other place in the world except this land of wonders they would be enshrined as a national monument, protected with fences and toll gates, and shown off with a nightly sound and light show. But in the Grand Canyon they loom in quiet splendor over the river, three huge caverns cut back into the vertical red limestone with marvelous smooth flat ceilings and floors that taper down to the river like open jaws. Even more remarkable is the group of slender columns that reach up from the sides and floors appearing to support the solid, perfect ceilings. As we drifted past I tried taking a few pictures from the water.

Then John, who was a few hundred yards ahead, shouted, "Hey, a boat!" Naturally we both had to land again to look at this new "find." It was tied to a tree, well up on the talus slope 50 or 60 feet above the water. It was painted a bright yellow, but as we got closer we could see that it was very weather beaten with open

---

*In 1952 the U.S. Bureau of Reclamation surveyed a potential damsite here. In the process they built a two-stage tramway from the rim to the river. The trip took over 20 minutes. It must have been a thrilling ride to soar out thousands of feet on a few strands of wire no bigger than the lump in your throat. No wonder they hadn't bothered to haul those pontoons out.

seams and cracked paint. It was about 15 feet long and had been well made once. On the foredeck was painted its explanation:

"BERT LOPER,
The Grand Old Man of the Colorado,
Born July 31, 1869 — Died July 8, 1949.
Near Mile 25"

"My God, he was almost 80—just a few days away from it. What was a man of 80 doing down here?"

John took a picture of me posed in typical tourist fashion sitting in Loper's boat, proving to no one in particular that I had been there. Then we left the old yellow boat to other canyon travelers and time.*

Our hated enemy, the wind, was acting up again, and the banks of the river were fuzzy with gathering sandstorms. We gritted our chattering teeth and were sorry we had stopped so many times. It was late afternoon and we still had ten long miles of slow water to Nankoweap. Now with the wind and shadow we could only look forward to a very uncomfortable afternoon, which could stretch into chilly evening.

Maybe it was that we were both so cold. So cold that we didn't converse, but just tried to hide from the wind and lose ourselves in a trance until the ordeal was over and we were in camp, warm and dry again.

---

*One or both of which took the boat—it is no longer there. Loper was a prospector and sometime resident on the banks of the river in the upper canyons. In 1907 he started with two friends on a run through all the canyons of the Colorado but lost his boat and his friends finished without him. In 1939, at age 70, he finally completed his run with a voyage through the Grand Canyon. On his second and last attempt in 1949 he overturned in 24 Mile Rapid, then apparently died of a heart attack. The next day his companions found his boat in an eddy and hauled it up on the talus slope.

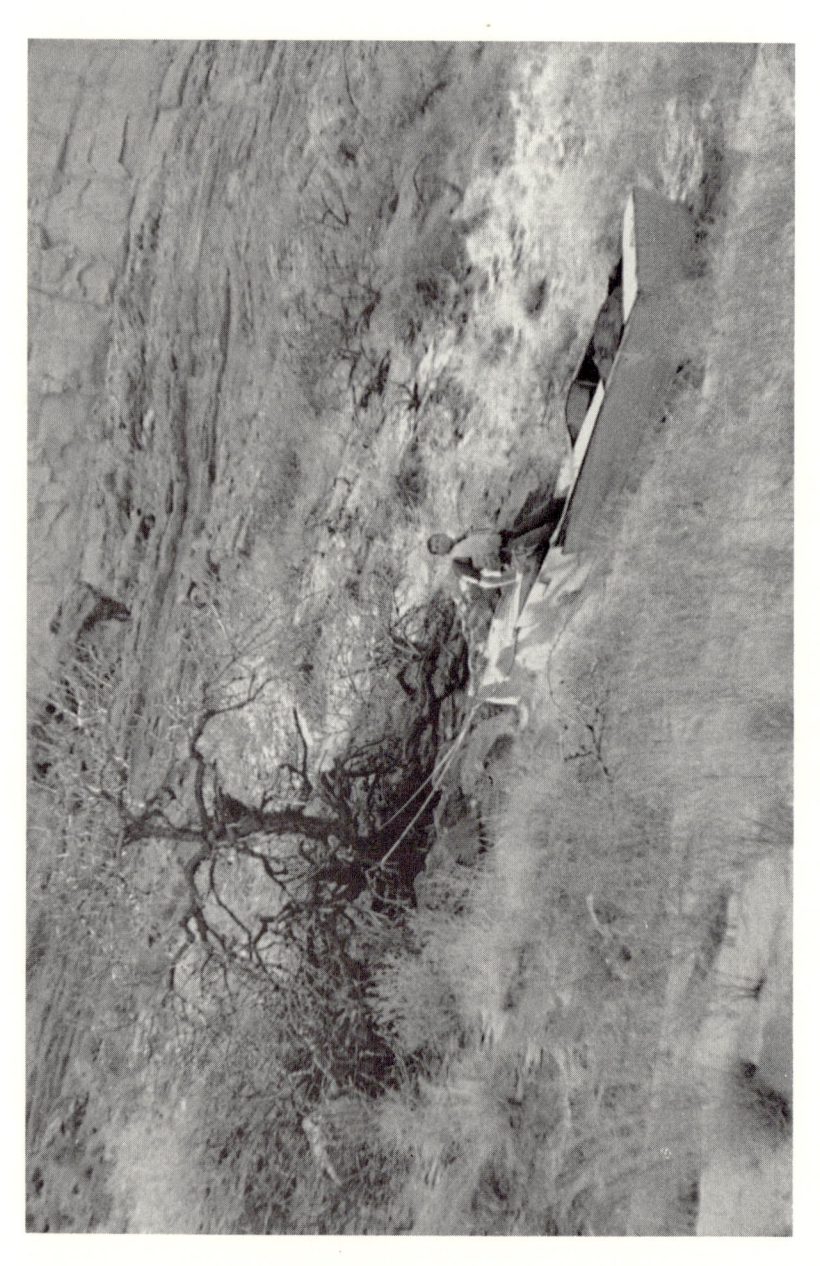

Bill examines a memorial to drowned river runner Bert Loper.

Maybe we had been too successful. In the last two days we had begun to boast to each other of how skillful and how tough we were and how the river didn't have enough rapids to satisfy us. Today had been particularly tame, we hadn't yet run a single rapids.

Maybe we would have been alert if we had known of the two graves above the river there. But we didn't, and nothing else broke our somnolence. We were just lucky it happened here and not at one of the far more dangerous places on the Colorado.

As we rounded the bend below Mile 43 we were greeted by the familiar sound of roaring water. I was about 150 yards ahead of John, so it fell to me to swim the rapid first.

President Harding Rapid isn't much of a rapid. Just a five-foot drop and not really rocky. Except for the big rock. That one is about as big as your living room and sits smack in the middle of the rapids. From a distance it doesn't look vicious. But as I came within a few feet of it I could see that its surface was water torn to the texture of a giant cheese grater with thousands of gouges worn into it — all separated by little knife-sharp ridges — small evidences of the great power of the river.

I passed through the rapid without incident, glad I hadn't rubbed shoulders with its big abrasive boulder, and turned back to wave to John to come through on the right side as I had. I continued to drift along backwards, watching John.

I saw him come over into the falling water headed straight for the rock. Or so it seemed. And then he disappeared behind it. I assumed that he had gone on the other side of the rock and wondered why he hadn't taken my advice and gone to the right. I drifted idly on downstream, away from the rapid, patiently watching the rock for John's expected appearance from behind it. Dimly at first, it began to come to me that he was taking longer than he should have. I wondered if he had been pinned to the rock. It hadn't seemed possible to me to climb out on it. I thought I had better not get too far downstream and began to swim toward the near bank. Then John's boxes appeared—suddenly—about halfway along on my side of the rock. John wasn't with them. I knew for sure that there was some kind of trouble and swam harder toward the shore.

I had almost made it to the rocky bank when John appeared on the surface about where his boxes had come up. He didn't seem to be moving or making any attempt to get to his boxes, which by now were some distance away from him. As I grounded my own boxes on a low, half-submerged patch of mud and turned to swim to intercept John I saw him closing in on his boxes and then reunite with them, clinging to one.

I yelled at him several times and was nearly waterborne when I heard him answer—weakly and unintelligibly. I paused. He was alive and conscious—and maybe all right. He was caught in a little eddy but didn't appear to be making any effort to get free of it. It was such a small eddy that there didn't seem to be any reason for him to be stuck in it. Then I noticed that his face looked very dark, sort of muddy.

Finally John freed himself and slowly, drifting mostly, drew closer to me and to the shore. I kept trying to figure out what was wrong with his face—then I saw that what I had thought might be mud was blood. He was bloody all over. There was blood dripping down his face and onto the collar of his life jacket. When he got within a few feet I saw that his blood was leaving a red stain in the muddy water.

I snatched onto his life jacket and helped him wade through the sticky, muddy shallows to a rock. he was dazed and, even with the red blood all over his face, looked pale. As soon as he was ashore he insisted that I get out my camera and take his picture; he rambled on that the first thing he had shouted to me when he came to the surface was to take his picture. It was to reassure me that he was okay—still his normal, hammy self. John was a little delirious, but since it seemed that he would do nothing till I had taken his picture, I fumbled out my camera and did as he asked—not even sure I had any film in it. The record taken care of, John sat down, propped himself against a rock and tried to tell me what had happened.

"I hit my head . . . look, my hand is laid open. Is that bone down there? I went under . . . under the damn rock . . . everything was all tangled up . . . my boxes were tangled up . . . my life jacket was pulling on me. I was dead. I was sure I was as good as dead. And I almost gave up and just waited. The river jammed me up . . . I couldn't move . . . I pulled with all the strength I had . . . then I hit my head . . . see? It's all bloody. It won't stop bleeding. I didn't have any air.

"But I came up. I don't know how it happened . . . it was wonderful! I was yelling at you . . . I wanted you to know I was all right . . . why didn't you take my picture? I told you to . . . I told you to three or four times . . . I was okay but I wanted to get a picture of big John right where he nearly got killed . . . did you get that picture I told you to get?"

I didn't know enough first aid to know how badly, but it was obvious that John was suffering from shock. He wasn't making much sense and his face was ashen. That word, ashen, is used so often that it means nothing. But when you see someone's face no longer pink, or tan, or even pale, but a gray ash color, it's the right word. Dead men look healthier than that awful ashes color.

I was hypnotized by John's ravings. I wanted the whole, blow-by-blow story of what had happened to him under that rock, but he wasn't making sense. He needed first aid, dry clothing and a warm fire more than anything else.

I took a look around—there was no place to camp here. What little ground was available was damp and there was no shelter from the wind. We were in a bend and couldn't see downstream. Since John couldn't get back into the water and we couldn't camp here, I would take all four boxes into the water to drift along the bank in hopes of finding a place to camp in the next two or three hundred yards while John worked his way along the shore.

John picked himself up and stumbled along the river's edge while I fumbled all four boxes afloat through the mud. I got free of the mud and quickly passed John, but as I was carried around the bend I could see that there wasn't going to be any campsite for us here. For almost three miles ahead the talus slopes on both sides started at the base of the cliff and plunged down at a steep 45-degree angle 200 feet directly into the river. There were no side canyons nor did the unbroken vertical cliffs reveal any of the amphitheaters we had used before. There wasn't so much as one square foot of level ground to lay a sleeping bag on. John had seen this too, and when I pulled ashore he was resigned to the fact that we had to go on.

This meant that John had to get back into the water. He could have picked his way along the sloping rock pile, but it would have taken hours of hard work just to climb along the bank for the three fruitless miles we could see ahead to the next bend. He wouldn't have been able to make it by nightfall. We were both reluctant to have him get back into the water, but there was no better alternative.

We drifted along slowly in the dimming light, searching every foot of both banks for a place we might have missed. There weren't any. Thank God John didn't have to move. His head and his hand wouldn't stop bleeding. He was just sitting between his boxes, holding his hand in the air, looking at it bleed and wondering why it wouldn't stop. The wind blew hard, adding intolerable insult to injury. It was blowing so hard that it was difficult to look ahead, and I searched for a stopping place in short stinging glimpses. John had given up and, turning his back to the wind, stared at President Harding Rapid as it grew faint in the gloom.

We came to the beginning of the bend and as we started round it we saw three more of the huge amphitheaters carved into the wall. These were Triple Alcoves and guaranteed us a place to camp. We landed near the first one and started to look for a suitable place.

John was a little more rational now and tried to help, but he was still bleeding and a little woozy so he soon went back to the river's edge and sat by the boxes.

There were about five acres of hilly jumbled sand and boulders below the cliffs. Thorny mesquite and cat claw seemed to grow in every level, sheltered spot, but I finally found a place in the little draw that led out of the central alcove. It was several hundred yards away from our gear, and when I got back I could see John was in no shape to carry anything. So I picked up one of his boxes and guided him to our campsite. Once there I built a fire and helped John off with his rubber shirt, never an easy job, but in this case more difficult because of his bleeding head. It had nearly stopped bleeding, but getting off the tight shirt started a new trickle.

After seeing John reasonably comfortable, I went off to bring up the other three heavy boxes. When I had finally made the fourth trip through the sand and rocks in my bare feet, then a fifth for water, I was exhausted.

We got a pan of water heated and John washed off the blood with many sighs and comments on the delights of washing in warm water again. With the blood washed off I took a good look at his wounds. One finger was ripped open to the bone, which was visible. I bandaged it, pulling the sides of the cut as close together as possible, then whittled a splint and bound the finger to it so he wouldn't be able to bend it and tear open the gash. Stitches would have been better I'm sure, but neither of us were willing to trust my sewing.

I took a look at his head. It looked pretty battered with many of the cuts under the hair, though few of them seemed too extensive. "These look too complicated," I said, "let's let them alone—probably heal better in the air anyway," Silently I wondered if they ought to have stitches, too.

While this was going on, John, by now rational, told me what had happened.

"I didn't think there was any danger," he said. "It looked easy. Compared to other rapids this one was nothing. When I saw that rock I hardly paid any attention to it, and even when I saw I was being swept right down on it, I didn't make any effort to swim out of the way. I knew I was going to hit. I figured at the last moment I'd push my boxes behind me and stick my feet out to fend off. Then I would just swing around the rock and pass on the same side you did.

"But it didn't work. All of a sudden I was swept under the rock."

"Under the rock?" I said, not quite sure how that could happen.

"I guess it was undercut—maybe shaped like a mushroom—with only the wide part showing."

That made sense; the top of the rock was out of the water most of the year, but the lower part was constantly exposed to the abrasive force of the Colorado, cutting away at it century after century.

"Well anyway, I got pulled under feet first, and suddenly there I was jammed up under this ledge. I couldn't keep on going because my boxes were caught somewhere and I was attached to them and my life jacket was pushing me up against the under side of the overhang. I struggled and wrenched back and forth, but I couldn't move much because the current had me pinned. Then I couldn't hold my breath any longer.

"You were under there a long time," I said.

"All I could do, I mean the only movement I could really make, was to pull on the line that went to my boxes. I pulled with everything I had; it was that or die.

"I hit the rock with my head and scraped along and then suddenly the river jerked me free and I came to the surface. I was really glad to get to the surface—I was so sure I was dead. Really. I was absolutely sure. Do you know what it's like to know this is your last minute? From now on I'm staying clear of those big rocks."

The river seemed to have assumed a new character. It was no

longer the easy not-what-it's-cracked-up-to-be lark we had been exulting about. All of a sudden, dramatically—almost disastrously—the river had become a dangerous thing.

Accidents or misjudgments might well continue to be rare for us, but the power and ferocity of the river guaranteed that if one happened it would be serious, possibly fatal.

John began to dwell on how helpless we were. Always before in our lives—at home, college, or the military—we had immediate and expert medical aid. Family doctor, school nurse, team doctor, battalion surgeon, all of these had been on call. Here in the canyon there was nothing but dirty old Bill or dirty old John with a few water-soaked band-aids. If wounded we couldn't get to a doctor, nor could we get a doctor to one of us for several days. If both of us should get hurt, we were helpless. Say the one going for help fell and broke a leg on the way, for example. These things we had distantly known from the start, but now we had to face them squarely.

It was a solemn pair that turned in that night.

And it was a pessimistic pair that woke up at dawn to the discouraging whisper of the wind, warning us that with such an early start, it would have a great time with us before this day was finished.

John was much better in the morning. His head looked awful—caked with blood here and there—but he felt okay. His hand was a little sore and of course the splint and wrappings rendered it nearly useless. But he managed, though I did carry his boxes.

By the time we were in the water, the wind was blowing in little gusts.

We stayed in the water for the five calm miles down to Nankoweap Creek; the juncture of the two streams marked one corner of the Grand Canyon National Park. Marble Canyon was now officially Marble Gorge, but it would be another dozen miles before we left its narrow, gloomy confines to enter the Grand Canyon proper.

Nankoweap has the biggest delta along the Colorado—all by

itself it has forced the river into a wide oxbow, most of which is one long rapid. The river drops 27 feet in one mile here. We climbed out on the upstream side of the delta, glad for the shelter it gave us from the wind, and walked over to the creek for a ceremonial drink. John looked at the acres of boulders that was the delta and observed that this place was probably pretty violent when both the Colorado River and Nankoweap Creek were in full flood. It must have happened sometime, for some of the boulders had been deposited where they lay by Nankoweap Creek, and others, hundreds of feet from either stream, showed the characteristic pockmarks created by the grit-laden Colorado. With the Colorado flowing this day at 7,300 cubic feet per second it hardly seemed possible that the river could multiply its volume by the 10 or 20 times necessary to reach so high. But we knew it did—almost every year—and had once reached a volume of 325,000 cubic feet per second. That was 45 times as much water as roared down the rapid at the moment. What a sight it must have been here when all that water poured through!

We couldn't find the cliff dwellings—actually we didn't look too hard. We were late, our feet were sore, the wind was sandblasting us, and yesterday's events had quelled our enthusiasms somewhat. Both of us felt we had a river to swim—seemingly no longer a trivial task—and we wanted to set about doing it. Fooling around with non pertinent side trips was secondary.

So we confined our explorations to a survey of Nankoweap Rapid. Nearly a mile and a half long, the rapid was shallow and foamed around the big bend like soapsuds being hosed down a staircase. We thought of our unpleasant bumping in Vasey's Paradise and realized the water was much faster here, but since the alternative of walking around always seemed to be more unpleasant than swimming any rapid, we shrugged our shoulders and wandered back through the wind and noise to our boxes nestled comfortably in the "quicksand."

We settled ourselves between our boxes and shoved off with a resignation. Neither of us will remember Nankoweap Rapid with any joy. We were bumped and banged and scraped most unpleasantly for the whole mile and a half—each contact with a rock came without warning and was perhaps more frightening than painful. Our relief at getting through with only a bruising didn't last long.

As soon as we were out of the rapid we were attacked by whirlpools. They had been lying there waiting for us and each of us was snatched out of the current, spun around and dragged over to the shore. We fought and cursed and struggled and when, now and then, one of us made a little progress downstream and turned to chide the other, a new whirlpool would seize upon this moment of hubris to swoop the triumphant one back upstream behind his miserable compatriot. We traded relative positions for more than a half hour below Nankoweap without making so much as a mile before the river tired of its sport and we were off again.

Off into the wind, which was now screaming up river at us, turning our world into froth and spray. In the long straight corridor the waves had a three-mile fetch and had built up to a height of two or more feet. Since our heads were about a foot out of the water this made for difficult visibility. And the tops of the waves were indistinct—as soon as one rose up the wind blasted off its top, turning the muddy water into fine buckshot which exploded into our faces. Our only recourse was to turn around and take these fusillades in the back of the neck. And wish we had a nice high and dry boat with a motor on it to ride in.

Kwagunt Rapid was a smaller copy of Nankoweap. Same little creek with a big delta, same long shallow rapid, same banged ankles and shins, same bloody whirlpools and screaming wind. We could hardly see where we were going and hardly cared anymore. When the next rapid came up the noise of the wind was so loud we were on top of the rapid before we realized it was there. This was 60 Mile Rapid and there was a rock in it suspiciously reminiscent of President Harding Rock.

I was ahead and kept to the middle of the river, planning to just miss the rock, but when John saw it he drove hard to the right and began hugging the shoreline. Like John in President Harding Rapid, I miscalculated the current and found myself headed straight for the rock. I swam with all my strength to avoid it, but couldn't make it. The river drove me right at the rock; I could only try what John had tried without success—to fend off with my foot. I, however, now knew the rock might be undercut so was careful to hold my foot above the water and push off on a piece of rock I could actually see. Like a football player with a stiff arm, I was able to pivot around on my leg and rush past safely.

John, of course, missed it by a country mile. He later told me that when he saw that rock he was scared, not because he really thought he'd be hurt—he knew he'd miss the rock—but scared just because it was there, like some people are scared of heights or the dark.

Except for that rock, this had been a day of long, windy, miserable miles. Why we didn't just stop and get out of the wind and say to hell with it, I'll never know. I suppose neither was willing to be the first to give in, and we were getting a little tougher and could take more of the river and the cold water, and we were still running behind schedule. For whatever reasons, we kept going long past tolerability.

The canyon was still growing deeper—we were about 3,500 feet down now. And while it was widening, the growing depth still gave us only about four or five hours of direct sunlight a day. The wind and cold water were bad enough, but in the shade they became almost unbearable. We hoped this problem would lessen once we were in the Grand Canyon itself, despite the Granite Gorges and their fearsome reputation.

We came to a place where the river seemed to widen and bend to the right, though the wind had rendered any observation questionable. As I started around the bend the wind seemed to increase. For as far ahead as I could see—at most a half mile—the whole canyon was a mass of spray and sand.

That was where my tolerance ended. Since it was too noisy to be heard, I waved to John to follow me and swam to shore. When he caught up he was told, "We camp here." His protests that we could still make more mileage weren't convincing—even if he had meant them.

Camp that night was one of the most unpleasant we spent on the river. The wind continued to howl and scream with increasing fury.

We found a little box canyon that gave some shelter—at least it seemed to slow the wind down a bit. When I started out to get some firewood I had to turn back; the sandstorm outside was so furious I couldn't keep my eyes open. Once again the useless face plate became useful, but not without also fully dressing and bundling my face and hands completely to protect them from the stinging sand. Even so, it was so difficult to see that I was forced to grope for firewood. It was difficult to stand up in the wind and with the tough terrain providing poor footing anyway, I found myself crawling about gathering chunks of driftwood on all fours.

Little wonder that camp the next morning was a mess. We didn't unzip our sleeping bags and roll out—we dug ourselves out. Little sand dunes had marched into our camp and stationed themselves around anything that was solid. Boxes, bushes, bodies and what was left of our woodpile were now soft little rolling hills of sand.

This Colorado River sand was not really sand but rather fine silt somewhere short of talcum powder in texture. It was the river's principal abrasive and was both the tool and the end product in the carving of the canyons. The river carried tens of thousands of tons of silt past us every hour—a half million tons per day was the accepted figure. It was continually picking up and laying down large and small beds of this silt. All along the edge of the river, back into the mouths of the side canyons, sometimes high on the cliffs or sloping walls of boulders, silt was laid out in sheets or clung in cupful amounts in every little crack. Even where cliffs dropped straight into the river, we could always see a little sprinkle of silt here and there on the sheer wall.

The silt turned the water of the river into a uniform brown, gritty to the taste, gritty to the touch—water that made your clothes dirty rather than clean. And when the wind blew, the silt turned the air into the same brown. This brown air filled our noses, our mouths, our ears. Silt ground into the cracks in our chapped hands and lips and made them bleed; by the sixth day out we both had raw fingers, tender and hard to use. It matted our hair and beards, rendered our food nearly inedible and nearly destroyed our cameras.

Along the edge of the river huge banks of silt, laid down by previous years' annual floods, collected wherever conditions allowed. In April the Colorado was gathering for its annual runoff when melting snows from the Rockies flooded the canyons. As the river rose it cut away at old silt deposits and we often saw or heard long banks of silt sliding into the water. At night they sounded like some prowling animal taking a moonlight dip. With no warning at all we would hear a long *swiiish* . . . then silence.

Some silt banks were dry and firm and would make excellent speedways, others had the consistency of syrup and we could almost swim through them. In between we found "quicksand" of all varieties. Sometimes we could stand on a crust of sand overlying a Jello-like substrate and by bouncing rhythmically up and down could get a half acre of silt to quiver and shake. Sometimes the crust would suddenly give way with a *schlurp* and we would be up to our hips in goo. At other times we couldn't step on a silt bank without slowly sinking in—once in a while we would become imprisoned and could only escape by lying out flat and slithering snakelike back to the water to try another route. Our swim fins were excellent for walking on the "quicksand." And, if we were careful not to stand in one place too long, we could get across much more easily with fins on than off. Once in awhile the stuff would grab a swim fin and try to tear it off our foot; this was scary only in that we had no spare fins.

The silt had two positive uses: it made excellent scouring powder for dish washing and we could mire one box in the stuff and, even if its attached mate were floating, never worry about the two drifting away.*

---

*It's sad that all that silt is now slowly filling up lovely Glen Canyon. But it's perhaps sadder to know that the huge silt banks, along with the huge driftwood piles, are now gone from Marble and Grand Canyons. The smaller banks are disappearing too, as the river carries off the silt but brings no replacement. The finer silt is long gone—today's river sands are only the coarser grains. Without the silt banks something alive and fascinating is missing from the Canyon.

5

The Big Canyon

The wind abated for awhile that morning and from high on a prominent bluff I could see across from us, coming out of a large side canyon, a thin streak of bright blue water—the Little Colorado River. Pity we hadn't been able to see well enough the night before to land on that side. We debated swimming over to have a look at it, the blue water was so pretty, but it would have meant we'd have a very hard swim just to land a half-mile downstream of the Little Colorado, leaving a long, hard hike back up.

Officially, at least, we were about to enter the Grand Canyon, although for about two miles below the mouth of the Little Colorado we were still in the fairly narrow canyons typical of Marble Gorge. The wind began to howl again and the sand was blowing. The river here was shallow so we contended with a succession of sand and gravel bars and islands and bumpy rapids, too busy to notice the slight widening of the canyon.

From any direction there is no real warning to the Grand Canyon—it bursts upon the hiker, the flier, the boater and the two swimmers with all its drama. After leaving the Little Colorado, the river sneaks south between a bulwark of terraced cliffs—to the east these cliffs reach abruptly to the rim, but on the west, behind nearby buttes, the Grand Canyon is already formed, invisible as yet from the river.

It was a jolt to be swept around Temple Butte into the Grand Canyon. Suddenly whole ranges of mountains lay in front of us. Stratified towers, gigantic beyond comprehension, filled the sky. Ten miles away the South Rim loomed up, then zigzagged off to the west for another hundred miles. The North Rim, another world of soft forests and lakes, was a mile above us.

Flowing with the river, looking out from only a few inches above the water, the very size, the immensity, of the place was astounding. But more overwhelming than its size was its beauty. Terraced mountains mirrored each other, matching layer for layer across the chasms, sweeping bands of pastel stone piled one on the other to press flat up against a pastel sky.

It all suddenly seemed so preposterous—our being there. Men have an enormous conceit that can usually ignore most realities. John and I had been thousands of feet down in the canyons for a week now, yet had refused to abandon a feeling that we two were the most important thing in the gorge.

Now we felt infinitesimal. Suddenly we were so small that we didn't matter at all. It was hardly important whether we continued or quit, whether we succeeded or failed, whether we lived or died. We were intruders who meant nothing, and all our thoughts and emotions of the past week were preposterous and presumptuous.

It was a disquieting feeling, contradicting a lifetime of egocentrism. But, strangely, at the same time we felt relieved of the burdens of our petty ambitions and frustrations—free to be just little dabs of protoplasm that would be gone tomorrow. It was a mystic experience in the classic sense, perhaps akin to the instant religious conversions some people experience.

So many people see the Grand Canyon and cannot believe

what they see. It is too much. They refuse to accept something so out of their range and they think or utter some flippancy like, "Golly, what a gully!" and go their way unaffected.

Others are irrevocably changed. Their feelings about the canyon amount almost to a form of worship. They join an unorganized but very real Canyon Cult whose members know each other, make regular pilgrimages, observe peculiar ceremonies and disdain the uninitiated.

Our entrance into this grandest of all places left too little time for reflection. As the canyon widened out so did the river. After dropping through Lava Canyon Rapid we were in a steep wide river. In many places it was two or three hundred yards wide and very rocky. Gravel islands appeared frequently and we seemed to be in one continual rapid. The river wandered back and forth in a series of oxbows, touching the now somewhat lower cliffs on one side and then turning back to run at the cliffs on the other side. We snaked back and forth with the river, fascinated at new sights with each change of course. We could see both rims, sometimes alternately, sometimes simultaneously, always distantly.

But the wind continued to blow, seemingly harder now in the more open canyon. And the water was again growing cold. Once again the familiar cry, "I'm getting cold."

And the usual answer.
"Already?"
"Yeah, let's stop."
"Let's go a little farther."
"Now!"
"After the next rapid."
"Oh, all right."

Since we were almost continually in rapids it wasn't hard to agree to the compromise and in a few minutes we were both in Tanner Rapid where the river takes a left turn, flowing tight into the cliff for the length of the rapid. At the foot of the rapid the first convenient whirlpool carried us a few feet over to a low ledge where we climbed out. It was an ideal spot for a break.

We were partly sheltered from the wind and piled on the ledge were two or three cords of wood for our warm-up fire. In minutes we had a bright bonfire. From where we sat we could see the Desert View Tower outlined against the sky on the South Rim. Tourists coming by road from the east get their first sight of the Grand Canyon there. We wondered if any of them noticed our fire or its smoke.

"If they see us, I wonder what they think it is?"

"Who knows? If that story ever got in the papers, they might have heard about us up at the Village. Somebody could guess we made the fire."

"Suppose the Rangers were watching for us . . . with binoculars or a telescope."

"That wouldn't be so great. They might come looking for us, try to stop us or arrest us or something."

"Aw, don't be silly, they wouldn't do that."

"You think they'd *like* having a couple of guys down here swimming what they consider a real dangerous river? Remember, they spend half their time pulling Joe Tourist up from the middle of the trail where he collapsed from extreme pain of the bunions. Do you think they want more work?"

"Maybe we shouldn't take the hike to the rim?"

We speculated for awhile about leaving the river for a brief hike up to Grand Canyon Village. We both could use more food—candy too. My rubber shirt was ripped and the rubber cement we'd brought didn't hold the patches on. I wanted a proper inner-tube-repair kit. John felt he could find room for a little more bourbon. On balance we were against the idea; if we did leave, we would be wise to sneak quietly up, take care of our needs and slip back down quickly.

Whatever we decided would have to wait until we reached the Bright Angel Trail 18 miles farther down river. Right now we were still behind schedule and must get back in the water and swim on.

The river continued to show its new characteristics: wide, shallow and bumpy. The river was flowing at the time at about 8,000 cubic feet per second. The waves made by the shallow river were enhanced by the wind and we bobbed up and down like cork floats. The first time we hit bottom in this bouncy water was a real shocker and we began to peer intently through the spray for stray boulders in midstream, but we soon adapted to the new conditions, stretched ourselves out flat and had no mishaps to speak of.

Until Unkar Rapid. It was a real rapid, dropping about 25 feet in a few hundred yards. We both got batted around pretty badly running Unkar. I had a frantic half minute of twisting to see where I was going, trying to straighten out my legs and body so they would be just barely beneath the surface, but getting slammed here and there nonetheless. Unkar wasn't one of the vicious rapids, even though we were both hurt a bit. The cold, at least, was analgesic.

Once again that cold and the wind combined to keep us from making our goal. It was very discouraging. Each day we started out with a definite minimum objective and we never seemed to be able to come within a mile or two of it. Again today we were both ready to stop early. I was most anxious, principally because of the leaking rubber shirt, but John was at least willing. So after bouncing out of Unkar, sore and numbed, we spotted, of all things, a clump of trees. They were really reeds and tall sage, but from the river they looked like trees. Whatever they were, they promised shelter from the wind.

Nestled in the reeds was a little lagoon, part of the river abandoned in last year's flood. It was the first time we'd been in a canyon wide enough to allow such a feature. Camp was to be a long way off the river so we both tried for the first time to carry two boxes at the same time. This meant struggling for 300 yards through mud and sand with about 150 pounds on our backs. I did okay — got about halfway before jettisoning one box—but old John, never satisfied with the unspectacular, knew he could make it if he took a shortcut through the reeds.

I was already in camp with my one box when I heard snorts, grunts and crashing like a wild boar rooting in a jungle. Then I heard, "Hey, Bill, which way is camp?" Before I could answer there came a crash, a splash, a moment of silence, then a long string of unhappy words. Minutes later John staggered into camp covered from head to toe in smelly mud with only one box. On his return trip to retrieve his remaining box and get us a bucket of clear water from the lagoon, he slipped and fell in, muddying the water he had to bring back. I demanded he return and bring back clear water — my small revenge for his own disinterest in my barefooted encounter with the rattlesnake a few minutes before.

After dinner I discovered that I had left my coffee behind at last night's camp, covered up by the blowing sand, no doubt. Giving up smoking was trial enough, but coffee too? Maybe taking the trail to the rim wasn't such a bad idea, after all. It was only a 5,000-foot climb and about a 20-mile round trip.

"We'll do it," John agreed. "I really don't want to run out of whiskey. And anyway, there's nothing like a little hike to break this monotony of swim, swim, swim all day long."

We again added up the cumulative effects of the "erosion" that was wearing away at us and had by now become a real problem. We had taken one week to swim 73 miles out of 280 and already wondered if we and our equipment were going to hold out. Both my ankles were rubbed raw and one had a serious slice; I had burned one foot, John had injured one knee; I had cut a couple of fingers and had a gouge out of my right palm, John had cuts on his head and still wore a splint on his finger; both of us had blisters on our faces from sunburn, chapped and bleeding hands and tender soles. Our cameras and pistols had repeatedly gotten wet and sandy and none of them were working too well. A strap on one of John's boxes was about to tear off and our long johns were popping

John repairing injuries

buttons and shredding in the seat. In short, we were a mess.

We resolved to use preventative measures: we would wear shorts over our long johns; we would get some softer grease, probably Vaseline, to fight the drying of our skin; we would religiously wear shoes around camp and be extremely careful in all our shore activities to avoid cuts, bruises, burns and abrasions. We had to begin treating our equipment with dedication, protecting everything from sand and ash and water. This meant being especially careful to seal our boxes properly, as well as sealing the plastic bags inside them. We would not permit the river to wash away more food, ruin more film, or destroy more equipment. Otherwise we weren't going to make it through the next 207 miles.

The day ended on a light note. I was fooling around with packing and happened to stuff a filthy undershirt behind the glass of my useless diving mask and discovered the combination made a perfect mirror. We spent a happy ten minutes snatching this makeshift looking glass back and forth and guffawing at our own unrecognizable selves. Dirty, cut, unkempt, unshaven, disheveled—we looked like the bad guys in a horror movie.

The next morning was a Sunday, just one week from the day we had gotten up early a few miles from Lees Ferry full of wonder and doubt about our trip. And now, though a little battered and beaten, we at least knew what we faced; we would meet the Colorado's war of attrition with a vigorous defense.

But we crawled out of our sleeping bags to survey another camp that had been made a mess of by the wind. We looked up at an overcast sky and felt the caress of an ominous early morning breeze. We slouched through a chilly breakfast without humor, not even laughing anymore at each other, though we were both covered with sand and ashes like Hindu holy men.

By the time we slopped across the damp mud flats to the forbidding river, cold and muddy, we both had the same feeling we had at Soap Creek. We wished we were someplace else. Getting in the water listlessly, we swam out to midstream and drifted around the bend. A mile below our camp we hit 75 Mile Rapid and 75½ Mile Rapid, which stretch out for about three-quarters of a mile. We had a busy time dodging rocks swimming to the right, swimming to the left, but got through with only minor buffeting.

A few miles below we came to what we thought was going to be the entrance to the Granite Gorge and Sockdolager Rapid. Its reputation was such that we had already decided to get out and survey it. We were again somewhat confused by landmarks and actually stopped at Hance Rapid.

And a good thing, too. Hance at the time, and at that stage of water, was undoubtedly the second most dangerous rapid on the river. It was certainly the worst looking thing we had seen so far. Its drop is 30 feet in half a mile—most of that 30 feet in its first 500 yards. Not only was it a big rapid with big rocks, but it was also shallow. There were more boulders showing than we had ever seen in a rapid—rows upon rows of them lined up in ragged ranks like a platoon of soldiers taking cover. The water raced through them at an outrageous speed, whipping itself into a continuous froth.

John and I had by this time become infatuated with the idea of swimming all the rapids on the river. So even faced with Hance and what seemed an impossible rapid, we didn't abandon our hope. Instead, we built a fire in the lee of some boulders and sat out of the wind listening to Hance's roar, ate an early lunch and studied the problem.

We had already avoided sets of two or three rocks by swimming busily in one direction and then another as we swept through a rapid. But here we were facing something really tough. There were so many rocks that we were not sure that we could get through without hitting a half dozen. We might dodge the first set and with a little difficulty could get by a second or third. But as we passed each group of rocks there would be an increasing likelihood that the dozens of counteracting and interacting currents would throw us off course or out of control. The possible mishaps multiplied with each rock. These were evil looking chunks of stone with jagged edges and sharp points where they had been broken by the mashing and grinding that continually goes on in the bed of the Colorado. Worse yet were rocks that we could see only now and then as a surge revealed dark fangs poised a few inches below the surface. The pieces of driftwood that we watched tumble through never followed the same course twice. And some of that driftwood had jammed up against boulders in the tumultuous water proving that we, too, might hit one squarely.

Rain clouds threatened and it sprinkled a little. The wind and sand blew without respite and the roar of the rapids was so loud we could scarcely hear each other. Then there was the ominous thought that in another half mile or so we would enter the Granite Gorge. Of all the tales we had heard about the river, the worst were reserved for the Granite Gorge.

After finishing lunch we walked about and looked at the rapid some more. We pretended to take great interest in the dikes and mineral deposits that showed on both sides of the river. We even found a little pocket of quartz or garnet in a boulder and tried to pick it out, but with no tools we only managed to chip away a half hour of our day.

John appeared pretty definite about not wanting to run this rapid, though he didn't say so. I felt sure that if I ran it, however, he would follow. Staring at the rushing water long and carefully I calculated that I could get halfway through the rapid easily and safely—still in control. But from there on the effect of cumulative minor errors was impossible to predict. I would be in the hands of the gods.

"Do you think you can make it, Bill?"

"Maybe not, but I'm going to try."

We discussed the rapid no further. Instead we planned how the movies John would make of the run would be taken. We made preliminary shots of the surrounding country, of the water and especially of some of the more wicked looking rocks as the river alternately covered and exposed their fangs.

I walked back upstream, taking more "last looks." The more I saw the less chance I thought there was of getting through safely. I wanted very much to swim this rapid—I had already swum fifty or sixty and wanted, like John, to swim all of them. When the thought occurred that the only good reason for swimming Hance was that I wanted to, and there were a lot of offsetting bad reasons—all those sharp rocks and that swift water—I changed my mind. I walked back to John and told him I thought we'd better drag our boxes along the edge of the river and get back in downstream of the rapid. He concurred and we went back to our equipment and started floating it along the boulder strewn edge of the river.

The boulders ranged in size from basketballs to automobiles and here at the edge of the river water strained through and around them at varying depths and speeds. We tried floating our boxes, tied in pairs, out on tethers and guiding or pulling them through this maze. But they always seemed to get jammed up somewhere or else swept out toward the swift water. We slipped and fell and pulled and jerked and helped each other and finally gave up. We had "lined" our boxes a hundred yards or so and hadn't yet gotten to the head of the rapid. We agreed that it was a fine way to get a broken leg.

"Set up the camera, John, I'm going swimming."

And with that I was out into Hance Rapid with a hard swim to get in the main current. And, of course, I didn't quite make it, bouncing off several boulders. But finally I reached the side of the main tongue and was off on the now familiar roller coaster ride. It was a long ride because just below Hance there was a second and then a third rapid. Or perhaps they were merely continuations of Hance. In the middle one I hit a rock very hard, first on the knee, then on the ankle, ripping a good patch of flesh off. "There's a scar I'll keep for a long time," I said to myself. It didn't hurt much thanks to the cold water, though I did limp for a few days afterward.

But there wasn't really much time to think; I was still in relatively shallow water and a couple more rocks kept me snapped to attention before I left the rapids.

As soon as I was out of swift shallow water and had a chance to look at my surroundings I realized I had entered the Granite Gorge. The canyon had narrowed considerably—an observation whose importance we were slow to realize. A narrower canyon of course meant a deeper river. And while the rapids here might produce great drops and horrendous waves capable of flipping boats and dumping passengers into the rapids, we who were already in the rapids had little to fear from the waves; the scarcity of boulders in our path, however, was a real blessing.

The walls were not sheer as we had become used to, rather they were a steep V shape, about a thousand feet high, making a canyon within a canyon. The Granite Gorge is narrow enough that we no longer had the wide vistas of the past day and a half and only now and then could see the rim. And the rocks were new to us, dark colored, gnarled and wrinkled and shot through with seams and pockets of lighter colored rock or minerals. Not granite—actually hard metamorphic rock—but the label sticks. Very little grew here, even the pockets of sage and cactus we had become used to were scarce.

We had read that campsites were difficult to find and rapids were difficult to survey or walk around, and as I looked down the narrow slot of the gorge the only horizontal thing I could see was the surface of the river itself. I saw no sandbars, no flat sedimentary ledges, not even any little pockets of silt in the rocks. The only campsites we were likely to find would be in the mouths of side canyons; even there we might find only boulders.

But we still had eddies and whirlpools. And now they were everywhere, not just below rapids. I swam into a convenient one to wait for John to catch up. He rejoined me in about 15 minutes, reported that he'd had no serious difficulty getting through the last series of rapids and, more importantly, that he thought he'd gotten good shots of my run of Hance.

▲ *In Los Angeles before departure we are asked to demonstrate our untested river- and rapids-swimming skills for CBS News.*

▼ *This rock near Lees Ferry has stood for eons but neither of us had the courage to roll out his sleeping bag under it.*

▲ *Left: Bill peers into an exploratory shaft bored into the walls of Marble Canyon for a threatened dam. Right: Only 38½ miles from Lees Ferry and already John must dry out his clothes.*

▼ *Left: John insisted that Bill take this photo a few minutes after he was nearly killed under President Harding Rock. Right: The morning after his accident at President Harding Rapids, John shows some of his wounds and his recovered strength.*

▶ *John stands on a corner of the larger boulder-strewn delta of Nankoweap Creek.*

▼ *Left: Bill studies the map at Mile 75 ½ to check that day's progress and the coming day's challenges. Right: In the morning at Mile 84 we discover we are camped in pink granite high off the river.*

▲ *A few of the scores of switchbacks on the Kaibab Trail — used mostly for cargo-carrying mules.*

▼ *Left: Bill, feeling like Huck Finn at his own funeral, poses with a morning headline at the top of the Kaibab Trail. Right: A solid grip on the rocks keeps the current from sweeping Bill past some good-tasting water.*

▲ *Clear water from Shinumo Creek joins the muddy Colorado River in dramatic fashion.*

▼ *From the South Rim of the Grand Canyon, the first sight either John or Bill had ever had of the Colorado River.*

▲ *Just upstream from Bedrock Rapid, Bill is a tiny speck in a huge canyon.*

▼ *Left: Bill, sitting on the straps connecting his rubber boxes, tries to warm up in the Lower Granite Gorge. Right: Bill rinses his muddy clothes in clear spring water sprinkling down the cliff at Fishtail Rapid.*

◀ *Lovely Deer Creek Falls plunges out of its crevice in the cliffs.*

▼ *The Indian word* Havasu *translates to "sky blue waters."*

▲ *John is almost lost from sight in the turmoil of Lava Falls.*

▼ *Left: We leave the Colorado River for the last time at Pierce Ferry. High silt banks show this place was once under Lake Mead. Right: A few miles upstream from Pierce Ferry we share congratulations and our last can of food.*

The Big Canyon

Getting through the granite became very trying. When the gorge narrowed a little the river whirled and boiled around angrily, slowing us down; and when it widened a bit and smoothed out, the river itself slowed down.

So when we came to the next rapid it was with relief at the chance to move along a little faster. This one was the famous Sockdolager of ill repute, but we didn't realize it at the time — to us it was just another big, booming rapid and a lot of fun. We were glad to have no boulders to dodge.

Our little strip of sky filled with threatening clouds, and the winds screamed and howled more fiercely than any we had yet endured. We had a full gale and then some. At least this time there was no sand in the wind, though the water droplets stung nearly as much. And it was beginning to grow dark. We had no idea where we were as landmarks were scarce here in the Granite Gorge. It wasn't hard to convince John to stop at the first suitable place.

The first suitable place advertised itself with a pile of driftwood about 75 feet off the water. It was perched on a little peninsula of rock that stuck out into the river and seemed to promise a small side canyon behind it. The current was swift here and we both began swimming hard toward the side as soon as we saw the driftwood.

Never in my life have I had a more frustrating incident.

I was no more than two feet behind John when he reached out and grabbed a projecting knob of rock. I missed it and was carried past him. Still swimming toward the cliff, I was able to touch the rock, but there was no convenient knob for me, and clutch and dig my fingernails as I might, the current still swept me away from the rock and downstream. Even a scant foot or two from the edge of the river the water was too deep to stand in.

With an anguished groan I was carried past the point of the little peninsula. Once around it I found a little side canyon, but try as I might, I could not swim into its mouth; instead, I was carried to the next little peninsula which formed the downstream wall of the side canyon. But as I approached the cliff there the current pushed me away from it toward midstream. A little frantic now, I swam toward the cliff has hard as I could and at last found a little whirlpool which allowed me to get next to the rock and jam my fingers into a crack. I still couldn't touch bottom, though. There was no place to ground my boxes, so I looped the tether line around my wrist and, finding a few hand and footholds, heaved myself out of the water onto the cliff.

I was now separated from John by only a few hundred yards. He had no idea whether or not I had been able to land at all. I yelled at him that I had landed and thought I could work my way back along the cliffs to the side canyon, towing my boxes through the water.

John yelled back at me, but we were too far apart and there were too many echoes for either of us to understand the other. The next thing I knew, there was John swimming around the point and into my whirlpool. He had come to help me. Unfortunately, he had his boxes with him, which meant he wouldn't be much help to me with mine. But as he said, he wasn't sure what my situation was, and he sure wasn't going to leave his gear even a hundred yards upstream in this impossible canyon.

So. To go on or not? It was dusk and we knew we had a sure campsite with a supply of wood not far upstream. We did not know how far downstream we had to go to the next possible campsite, or even if we could find one before dark. Swimming in the dark with rapids ahead was very unappealing. We could hear the next one roaring faintly from somewhere downstream, so we elected to struggle back upstream.

And a struggle it was. Swimming was impossible—so was carrying our boxes along the cliffs. We tied the four boxes together, swim fins lashed atop, and with one line leading up from them we inched along the cliffs, rock climbing in bare feet, taking turns towing or just holding the boxes against the hundreds of pounds of pressure the river exerted against them. The rocks were alternately slippery or sharp, the thin line cut into our hands, and hand and footholds were scarce. We cursed and yelled, sometimes at the cliff, sometimes at the river, sometimes at each other. We pulled and climbed and clutched till our muscles screamed back at us. Darkness came and we were still clinging to the cliff. Both of us had bleeding fingers and toes. John was tired, I was exhausted.

Somehow we made it to the little side canyon only to find there was no wood there. Furthermore, it wouldn't have been the place to be if a flash flood struck at night. Even so, we went for firewood, climbing up the cliff by flashlight.

Incredibly enough, up near that pile of wood we had first spotted we found a dreamlike campsite. Nestled in room-sized potholes in the rock were several level patches of clean sand. Nearly a hundred feet off the river we had four or five of these rooms, a couple with built-in fireplaces, created from smaller potholes cut into the rock walls—one even had a flue. Here and there were little potted plants growing in niches. Cut through the beautifully colored walls were windows looking out over the river. We were each able to choose his own bedroom with fireplace and view and blessed shelter from the wind.

We didn't try to carry all our gear up to our fairyland campsite, choosing to unpack in the side canyon. That is when I found the river had gotten into my gear and soaked everything I owned; so much for that morning's resolutions about careful packing.

The next morning's resolutions didn't fare much better. Our agreed plan was to swim to the Kaibab Suspension Bridge a few miles down river, cache our gear, hike to the rim, buy our supplies quickly and slip back down to the river before nightfall.

The first setback was finding that all my gear spread out to dry had been nearly buried by a layer of sand left by the wind. John was taking a few movies of this disheartening spectacle when the second scene suggested itself. Some of the cans in the bottom of my boxes gave dramatic witness to the effectiveness of our rubber boxes as bumpers, and to the buffeting to which we and our equipment had been exposed. So we shot a little scene of me holding these bent and beaten cans. One can in particular had been pounded nearly square.

As we tore open the sealed foil of each pack of movie film we realized that Kodak's nearly perfect protection was gone forever; the thing to do was mail this exposed film from the Village. Obviously we ought to shoot a little more film now when this opportunity to guarantee its safety was at hand. So we took a few shots of landing in the wind, bent cans, sandy gear and one marvelously overacted scene wherein I got to express extreme dismay at all these torments.

And since the wind was a handicap, necessitating shooting during lulls between gusts, the whole thing took a lot of time. It was past noon before we were ready to leave.

The wind was by now ferocious. On the way to the bridge we passed through places where the river narrowed to only a hundred feet or so, forming a venturi tube through which the wind funneled with hurricane fury. I guessed velocity in the gusts to be about 75 mph.*

We swam several rapids and were glad the deep narrow canyon had removed the danger of rocks. The wind was so fierce and the spray in our faces so blinding, we both thought it no better than swimming in the dark.

When the slender web of the Kaibab Suspension Bridge burst into view, it was a welcome sight. Here, where the mule and hiking trails from both rims met at the river, we were in contact again with the outside world. All we had to do was climb the 4,500 or so feet to the South Rim and to Grand Canyon Village, elevation 6,900 feet — an eight-hour hike, the books said.

---

*In fact, this date recorded some of the highest winds ever in the Grand Canyon.

6

Caught in the Act

We landed just under the bridge, opened our boxes (everything in mine was all wet again) and changed our clothes. John had a pair of dirty, wrinkled grey flannels and a suede jacket with a hole in it. I settled for jeans and a sweatshirt, both wet and dirty from their latest soaking in the muddy Colorado. We looked like fugitives.

We clambered up the cliffs to the bridge. As we crossed it, John was 25 or 30 yards ahead. When the big gust hit, the bridge buckled and swayed so much he was lost to view by the hump in the floor. I shrieked a warning and ran back; John kept on going. A minute or so later I raced across in a lull. John couldn't understand, and when I related the story of the Tacoma Narrows Bridge in Washington, which had tumbled from just such forces in the late 1940s, and explained what a close call we had had, John said, "After all the close calls this week, you let such a silly thing frighten you. Bill, I think that's the first time I've ever seen you really scared."

I wasn't so sure it was the first time, but I had been scared. I didn't like being 70 feet up on a spider web swaying in a hurricane.

It was more evidence, though, of the winds we had faced.

A short way up the trail we met a man—our first contact in a week—and we stopped to pass the time of day. Our disgraceful appearance made him curious.

"You fellers come from up the Kaibab Plateau?"

"No, down the river."

"In boats?"

"No."

"You walked? Supposed to be impossible."

Oh, what the hell. He's all by himself. Let's see what happens.

"No, actually we swam."

His eyebrows went up to his hairline. "Hey, you must be them fellers they was lookin' for."

"Looking for us?"

"Oh yeah, you two fellers is them fellers that is swimmin' in the river. They was lookin' for you all right. Yeah, lots of 'em. When you get to the top, ought to go in and see the Rangers. They wants to talk to you."

Oh lordy.

We quickly promised to see the Rangers and gleaned a little trail information from this good fellow. He said we had a choice of the nine-mile Bright Angel or the seven-mile Kaibab Trail. His preference was the Kaibab, even though there was no water anywhere. There would be few, if any, people on it.

So we chose the relentless 13 percent grade of the Kaibab. I set a fast pace which John tried to exceed by cutting off the corners of some of the switchbacks. We took our first stop at the top of the granite. As we looked down at the river we realized that we had just climbed 1,300 feet non-stop, higher than the Empire State Building—which, if placed on the river, would not reach as high as we were standing. We still had the equivalent of more than two more to climb.

The Kaibab is the newest of the dozens of trails which have been built from time to time in the Grand Canyon. Most of these

The view across the Kaibab Suspension Bridge – photo taken in a calm

were built for commercial purposes. Most are now in disrepair; some are impassible. The Kaibab was a government project built in 1928 at a cost of $147,000. With its north branch, it constitutes the only all year rim-to-rim trail left. It was engineered with an unvarying grade, to achieve which, sections had to be blasted out of solid rock, tunnels sometimes resorted to.

Along the trail the Park Service had set out signs to inform the traveler about formations, vegetation, fossils, etc. At about a half mile above the river we were informed by one that we were leaving the Lower Sonoran climate zone—the zone of the river and of places like Death Valley and the deserts of Mexico. We would pass through another two zones before reaching the forested rim.

We began to slow and John, who had at first complained I set too fast a pace, soon passed me. I was unable to keep up, even though we took more frequent rests. John found himself waiting for me at every place he could find shelter from the now cold wind. Finally he declared he could wait no longer—every time he stopped he got chilled and he was afraid he'd get cramps. So finally he gave me the nearly empty canteen and said he'd see me at the top.

That last thousand feet was agony. I had had no lunch and with every step became more fatigued. I could count only 50 steps before I had to stop, then 25, then counting became fruitless. Soon I was climbing in a state of semi-consciousness; when I stopped I didn't try to get off the trail—just fell flat into the mule manure. The water in the canteen ran out.

Darkness swelled slowly up from the canyon bottom, drowning the light and I had to concentrate on touching the cliff on one side of the trail so as not to fall off the other side—sometimes a several-hundred-foot drop. Any little hollow or pebble in the trail could trip me and make me fall. Often after a fall I crawled a bit, too weak to stand.

Thirst pushed me on. I knew that if I made it to the snow I would have water, but when I finally got to the first patch I nearly passed it—I may have been stumbling along with my eyes closed. The snow was refreshing and helped me make it to the rim where I staggered out onto the road.

There was no John. The man on the trail had said it was only two miles from here to the lodge—level miles, I hoped—but it was closer to four. While I could walk all right on the level, every little rise nearly finished me. It was absolutely dark by now and snow was falling. In spite of my plaintive signaling, all the cars passed me by. With only a sweatshirt, I was both freezing and frantic. I almost hurled myself in front of the next car. Which stopped.

After a few grateful words to the honeymoon couple in the car and my explanation that I had nearly done myself in hiking up the trail the question came:

"You didn't by any chance come down the river?"

Odd question out of the blue.

"As it happens, yes," I answered.

"Swimming?"

Oh lordy, again.

No point in lying. "Er, well, yes."

Then both at once they told me they had just heard the news on the car radio. There had been an all-out search for us—airplane and everything—and we had been officially given up for dead.

Dead?

As this kind couple and I walked into the Bright Angel Lodge together, people stared. Before joining my saviors at dinner I went to wash up and learned why. Looking back at me from the mirror was the worst looking man I'd ever seen. The river, the trail, the snow, the hunger and the fatigue had all done a real job on me. Washing made no change.

I had just finished my meal when John walked in with a distinguished looking man and sat down. I rushed across the room.

"John, where did you go?"

"Hi, Bill," John said nonchalantly, and introduced me to the manager of the lodge, Mr. Kennedy.

"Mr. Kennedy here has been telling me we're famous."

John then explained that he hadn't waited at the top of the trail since if I had needed help he had to be someplace where there was some to send. If I hadn't shown up in another hour or so, he planned to send someone.

"What's this *famous* stuff?" "I heard we were on the news."

Mr. Kennedy related a tale of newspaper stories in California and said that the Park Rangers, the County Sheriff and others had been alerted to watch for us. Then Victoria Graham, a long-time family friend of mine, had become very worried and insisted on hiring a plane to look for us. Of course, the plane couldn't fly low in the canyon because of the high winds, so naturally they had seen no sign of us. The papers had gotten hold of that, some official had made a fatuous statement and now the media were trumpeting our tragic deaths.

We had to make immediate efforts to resurrect ourselves. Our poor families. On the way to the phone booths I spotted a newsstand. Sure enough, the banner headline read, "FEAR PAIR LOST IN COLORADO SWIM TRY." In the article was a quote from the Ranger who had flown in the airplane. "They wouldn't have much chance, the Colorado is known as one of the most treacherous rivers in the world. Even experienced boatmen treat it with respect."

I wondered if he knew that we, too, happened to have a hell of a lot of respect for that river at this time.

Feeling a little like Huck Finn at his own funeral I began making long distance calls, with John in the next booth doing the same. My parents and brother and sisters were holding a wake with consoling friends when my call came through. Their reaction to the operator's request to accept a collect call from Bill Beer was typical of all those I placed. At first, suspicion that it was a crank call, then a whoop and everybody shouting into the phone at once.

There were those like my little brother and sister, John's mother and several of our friends, who had simply known the news stories couldn't be true; but some people had believed and were shaken to hear first that we were dead, then alive, in quick succession.

Turns out that the movies Dave had taken of our departure had been developed by a friend and turned over to television following up on the original stories we had given out ourselves. Then Dave had given a newspaper interview, others had added comments and the "search" had proven futile. With all that the story had had several days' play and had simply gotten a little bigger each day.

The next thing we knew the phone calls began coming back in. From the press. With all the hubbub there was no hope of our getting our meager supplies and going back down this night—it was nearly midnight. Mr. Kennedy apologetically offered us the hospitality of the Fred Harvey Company, saying he regretted the best room in the house was already taken.

John and I looked at each other and laughed. It seemed ridiculous that anyone would even offer us their back porch, much less the best room. We accepted gladly. We were nearly broke, anyway. A magnificent hot bath and a night between clean sheets were most welcome and the next morning we were treated to a sumptuous breakfast surrounded by genial business-suited executives of Harvey.

I think just watching us eat had to have been an event. Our appetites were enormous. Both of us ordered the largest breakfast on the menu then proceeded to eat a second and a third and finished off our orgy with a few donuts and coffee.

Things got a little sticky after breakfast. More phone calls came in, more questions. I reminded John that we just came up for some rubber cement and things and maybe we ought to slip away. He agreed, but as we strolled not very inconspicuously through the lobby a loud voice called, "Oh, Mr. Daggett! Mr. Daggett, long distance!" The Ranger perusing the new morning headlines about us at the newspaper rack turned abruptly.

Torpedoed!

Abandoning John to his phone call and hoping his ingenuity

could extricate him, I whispered that I'd meet him down on the trail, popped out the door, and hurried off to the safety of the store.

I made all our purchases and had just stepped outside when I heard, "Hey, Bill."

Across the street John was getting out of a squad car with a Ranger.

Sunk!

It was an event we had tried to avoid from the birth of the idea. Now we were both . . . in custody. We were escorted to the Chief Ranger. Then to the office of the Superintendent. There, surrounded by the top brass of the United States Park Service and Coconino County, Arizona, we faced . . . The Law.

And these guys were serious, judging by their faces.

The inquisition began without ceremony.

"You boys have given us a lot of trouble. I guess you know that."

Injured innocence. "Who, us? How?"

"You should have told us what you planned. Every party that goes into the Canyon is required by The Law to leave word at Ranger Headquarters. If people tell us their plans we are able to help them."

Sounded to me like one of those "three biggest lies"—the one that goes, "I'm from The Government; I'm here to help you." Obviously John thought so too, because he said, "Do you mean you would have given us permission?"

"Well . . . not necessarily. We don't normally do that."

Q.E.D.

The Kindly Old Superintendent went on to tell us what expense and embarrassment the Park Service had been put to in the matter of Beer and Daggett. People looked to the Service as Guardians of the area, and they had been forced to admit that they had no knowledge of us, nor our plans, nor our activities. The Park Service had been unable to answer criticisms or questions and there had been a good deal of both. Even from *Washington, D.C.*

Caught in the Act

They were good men, mostly. They were sincere, intelligent, dedicated and courteous.

It soon became evident from their tone that they were not really angry at us, nor did they intend to punish us. Consequently, the conversation grew less guarded and cautious and more friendly. The Rangers and Sheriff and other officials had many of the same questions the press and our families had had. Questions about our methods, our experiences, our conclusions. The Kindly Old superintendent signaled the end of the interview when he said,

"Now that you boys have had your fun, what are you going to do next?"

Oops.

"Well . . . ah . . . um . . ."

"You *are* finished." Not a question, a statement really.

Silence.

Then I mumbled, "Not exactly, sir. We still have about 192 miles to go, more or less, that is."

The conversation took on a new life.

There was *no way* they said. We were finished and might as well make up our minds to that, thank you. When we tried to object they took the gloves off with overtones of putting us in jail if we tried to sneak back down to the river.

We mustered every argument we could think of.

We said it was perfectly safe—overrated dangers and all that.

They cited drownings they knew of—including *Rangers*.

We claimed we were expert swimmers and cited all kinds of exaggerated qualifications to prove it.

They said so what.

We stated we were in magnificent condition and cited our three-hour climb of the Kaibab Trail to prove it.

They could relate to that and weakened a little, but still said no.

We were thinking so hard and talking so fast we began to perspire; I could feel a trickle running down inside my sweatshirt. We even pleaded we had to go down to the river to retrieve our gear.

They would provide an escort. Probably armed.

Then almost simultaneously, John and I conceived the crusher.

"You gentlemen realize that after all this silly publicity and stuff, you won't have a minute's peace until someone does swim down this river."

Stunned looks.

"Absolutely! There's hundreds of guys on Southern California beaches just looking for some way to get in the record books."

"Probably thousands. We met one guy who wanted us to wait a few days so he could come along on this trip."

A slight nod or two. A hemming and hawing.

"When all those guys hear we've been stopped after getting this far, they'll be up here in droves, jumping in the river from everywhere, drowning all over, cluttering up the landscape."

One Ranger seemed to turn pale.

"And it won't stop till someone does swim all the way. No matter how many die."

"The more drownings, the more that will try."

"You gentlemen have a big job ahead. A lot of patrols to make."

"Night and day, too."

There was a little buzz as all the uniforms turned to each other with nods and muttered acknowledgments. "You boys might be right there," the Chief Ranger said.

We bore in. "We sure are."

"And who has a better chance to finish it than us."

"We've been in the river for a week."

"We've swum all the rapids so far."

"We've tested and proved our methods, our equipment and ourselves."

"Our chances of getting through are really good—certainly better than someone just starting."

"Letting us go on could really save you a lot of trouble."

That bit of logic struck home.

After some discussion, Park and other authorities said that while they couldn't give us official sanction, they wouldn't really try to stop us.

Big smiles. Great relief.

We shook hands all around. John and I promised to keep the Park Service fully informed all the rest of the way; they would no longer have to admit ignorance of our doings. On the way out the Chief Ranger told us what he knew of the river we had yet to face. He said the "worst stretch" of the river followed Bright Angel Creek: Horn Creek Rapid; Hermit Rapid, where three people—including two Rangers—had drowned; and farther down, Lava Falls, supposedly the meanest rapid on the river.

On the way back to the lodge, rather than feeling triumphant about our success at keeping our project from being derailed, we were truly feeling a little chastened about the trouble we had caused the Park Service. They were really fine people and we had certainly caused them more trouble than they deserved. Like the Coast Guard, they help people day in and day out who give them nothing but trouble in return. Their good advice is often ignored by wiseacres who then get in trouble and think nothing of demanding the immediate assistance of the entire Park Service. We were truly sorry to have given them trouble. But more than that, we admired the courage of the Park Superintendent who knew better even than we did how right we were in our assessment of events that would have followed his restraining us. And who certainly knew better than we what troubles and criticisms *he* would have to face if we did drown.

The excitement of last night and today was finally too much. We were anxious to get back to our river and the job at hand. We made hasty farewells at the lodge, accepted a ride to the Kaibab Trail and started down nearly at a trot.

On the way down we met a mule train coming up. We stood aside so as not to spook the new mules, who were being broken in to Grand Canyon work by carrying freight, not people. As the driver passed, John asked him if he had seen the flashlight John had dropped on the way up the day before. The mule skinner promptly produced the flashlight. Wonderful country, with people to match.

We made it to the river in little over an hour. It was fast going, but we felt no real fatigue, save for a slight shakiness in the knees. We were glad to be back, but the river wasn't about to permit a truce in our little war. As I was repacking my boxes a rock rolled down the cliff and smashed my finger.

With throbbing digit aloft, I followed John into the icy water. We hardly had a chance for a backward look at the bridge before we were swept around the bend of Bright Angel Rapid. Another rapid followed quickly and then another. The extra length of the rapids and the riffles in between, which are characteristic of low water, made it hard to keep track of how many rapids we were swimming. After shooting through a fourth rapid we came to a half-mile respite. We were delighted. If this was the kind of river we faced, we were really going to have a crazy 190 miles. Horn Creek Rapid was next and it, too, was a wild, roaring ride.

We called a halt about five miles below Bright Angel to make some readjustments in packing; my gear was still damp from two days before and there was that rubber shirt to patch. We estimated that the last five fun miles had only taken about a half-hour to travel, which meant the river was moving at an average of ten miles per hour, faster in the rapids, slower in between.

It had been fun being famous for a few hours, but it was good to be back in the solitude where the river and the rocks didn't care who we were. That night we sat around our campfire speculating on what would happen to us after we came out of the Canyon. We were pretty sure we wouldn't be able to just go back to our apartment and take up where we had left off, but beyond that . . . ?

It was a night for contemplation. Overhead the desert sky was a wide ribbon of bright stars. On either side of this sparkling ribbon the dim outlines of the cliffs seemed to drop from the sky to my sleeping bag. Somewhere an invisible moon hung just outside of our little enclosed world. The flickering fire popped and sparked and the quietly slithering river added faint sounds of rapids and an occasional shoosh of falling sand banks. I began to see our venture as an allegory. We were on a course from which we could only deviate slightly, and like the course of a man's days, the river wandered and fluctuated, offering troubles and joys, calms and turbulences, but always it went on and there was no other way to go.

We knew the end—we had maps which told us of the landmarks—but each new day brought its own suspense. Other people had passed this way before and had told us of their experiences; but like children, we had to do it for ourselves. On the river, as in life, we had to meet and overcome each obstacle as it arose, making a little progress each day. There were times when we could have taken the "easy" way, but by doing so we'd have robbed ourselves. The river is measured in miles, life in years, but the real landmarks of each are accomplishments. We measure ourselves by how difficult our problems are and how well we solve them. Though John and I were in the early maturity of both our voyages, we could not rest on how much we had learned and accomplished to date. There were too many challenges ahead. The voyage is always fascinating to the end.

7

"This River Is Out to Get Me"

We arose that morning still elated by our visit to the rim, and at the absurd thought that while we were puttering around in our damp, grimy camp several million people were reading in their newspapers and hearing on their radios that the "intrepid swimmers" were continuing on their trip. Sore yes, cold yes, dirty yes, but intrepid . . . ?

Pity there was no one to watch the two "celebrities" as they stumbled down the sand to consign themselves to the raging waters of the Colorado.

And rage they did! What a day! We had nothing but rapids all day, with no time in between to take pictures. Salt Creek Rapid, Granite Falls, Hermit, Boucher, Crystal, Tuna Creek, Sapphire and several smaller ones followed one after the other. These were some of the big rapids of the Granite Gorge we had heard so much about. As far as I was concerned, they deserved a reputation but not the one they had; I had wonderful fun bouncing down these rapids like a rubber ball down a flight of stairs. I yelled and laughed and the canyons shouted back until at times I sounded like a whole carload of people screaming on a roller coaster. It was a wonderful sport. I wanted to swim every rapid in the world! We no longer stopped to survey rapids; they seemed not to offer any real hazards to us.

Even though I was feeling no fear, there was still excitement and tension just before going down the brink of each rapid when I could hear the noise but all that was visible was the smooth edge where the river disappeared. Both John and I commented on that tense "before the game" feeling.

And, just as before a game, the tension was always accompanied by a need to empty our bladders. It didn't take us long, however, to learn to wait till *after* the rapid before doing that. With long johns on we found that the process infused a temporary warmth that would insulate part of us from the cold river for a few minutes—if we didn't move much. John grinned, "It's almost as good as a warm-up break."

In camp that night we calculated we had swum ten miles and had dropped 130 feet.

John said, "I feel like it."

Poor John hadn't shared in the fun today. All day long he had been bouncing off rocks, proving they weren't *that* far below the surface. He never hit too hard, just enough to give him a bruise or take off a little skin. His camera, lunch, and both his boxes had sprung leaks, so he had another night of laying out everything to dry. He had removed the splint, and his finger had opened up again; now it looked as if he'd wear the new splint till we were out of the river.

The next day, the river started out on him again. In the first rapid he dropped down a wall of water onto a rock that scraped his foot and dislodged his swim fin. Panicky, he reached down to rescue the fin and was somersaulted over the rock into the hole be-

"This River Is Out to Get Me"

hind it. Still doubled over securing his swim fin, he was dumped onto another rock. And when he finally got the fin on and lifted his head for air, a wave squirted into his mouth and he inhaled a fair amount of muddy water. He coughed all the way to the next rapid.

The sun was shining brightly and there was, thankfully, no wind. It was far and away our most pleasant day so far. The water had warmed up to 56 degrees, not exactly warm, but we had finished the first hundred miles now and were a little tougher and tolerated it better.

Late that morning we stopped to look over an old cable car that spanned the gorge.* We thought it might be fun to see if we could get the 50-year-old device to operate well enough so we could run the car out to midstream and dive off, but it was rusted too solidly. We contented ourselves with a few photos and returned to swimming.

Around the next bend we saw Shinumo Creek, with its clear water coming into the river, and stopped again—this time to try taking some movies. Our damaged camera would no longer run by itself, but John figured out a way to jam a twig into the button so we were able to shoot a scene with both of us in it at once. Of course we didn't hear the spring wind down, so we carried on with our acting long after the camera was dead. Swimming down the Grand Canyon may not have been a silly thing to do, but how about two guys hamming it up in front of a dead camera?

Below Shinumo we raced through another series of rapids, dropping 50 feet in two and a half miles. Earlier that morning I had dropped into a big hole in one of the rapids and had come up bubbling that I had fallen into the "biggest one yet." But below Shinumo I seemed to find a hole in every rapid, each one bigger

---

*The cable car was built by William W. Bass, a miner, developer, tour guide, conservationist and all-around fascinating early canyon resident. The cable car, built to hold horses, connected the two halves of the first rim-to-rim trail. The cables have since been removed as a hazard to low flying aircraft!

than the last. In Waltenberg Rapid, I believe it was, I was swallowed by a real whopper. After I came out of that one I was dizzy. I'd read estimates of the depth of these holes that ranged up to 35 feet. Even half that is an outrageous lie. A really big hole is perhaps only ten feet deep. But it still takes plenty of power for a river to suck a hole in its surface ten feet deep, and there's a lot of violence all around the holes. They often overturn a large boat in a trice, but the poor swimmer doesn't get overturned—he gets rotated.

After that last ride in the Colorado's cement mixer I was ready to take a break. So when we saw the granite wonderland the cliffs had become, we swam ashore. The water that was again in John's boxes caused us to stay. It seemed a perfect place to do some serious filming, too.

All around us the irresistible forces of erosion had been resisted by hard stone, producing acre upon acre of sculptured forms. Fluting, it's called. The whole mountainside was one mass of smooth surfaced, softly convoluted shapes. Bare of foliage, the Colorado had created its own flora in everlasting stone. There were toadstool shapes, fern shapes, trees with delicate "granite" leaves and here and there vines of "granite," no bigger around than your finger, festooned from rock to rock.

The rock was shot through with quartz and other mineral seams. Your eye could follow these as they appeared and reappeared in adjoining clusters of rock sculpture as far as you could see. Here and there a seam of glittering mineral stretched across a patch of sand like a fine crystal plate buried with only the edge showing. In places, light shone through thin rock giving it the appearance of stained glass. The oblique afternoon sunlight was mirrored from crystals and facets all through the cliff so that the rocks twinkled.

We worked till nearly dark staging a "typical" camp sequence for the camera, then quit for the real thing. Our little wonderland made a fine campsite, complete with a carved stone fireplace which had its own hearth, mantle and flue. After we had draped our dirty

"This River Is Out to Get Me"

wet clothes all over it I wondered if perhaps we weren't taking too many liberties with Mother Nature.

She must have thought so, too. It was obvious the next morning that she was angry with us. We awoke to a cloudy, blustery, threatening day. It had been raining somewhere. Overnight the river had risen two feet and then dropped back one. With no banks to overflow, the Colorado just keeps rising in flood. We had passed clusters of driftwood deposited 75 feet up on the cliffs and knew the river had once reached that height. We could only guess how high and how fast it might rise overnight and hope we camped high enough above the water.

We were slow to finish our camping sequence the next morning. Considerable discussion—sometimes vigorous—over every single shot delayed us. It wasn't that were were angry, just cheap. Neither of us was willing to waste a single inch of expensive 16mm color film on a superfluity. As we worked, argued, and planned that morning, and as the camera was unloaded and reloaded several times, I couldn't help remembering the repair job I had done on the camera in Marble Canyon and wished devoutly that I could find out whether or not we were making blank film or movies.

By the time we got in the water it was raining; soon it began to rain hard. The rain was freezing, and I couldn't understand why it wasn't snow or hail. Almost immediately we agreed to warm up at "the first pile of driftwood after the first rapid."

But there were no rapids. For miles. It became a contest to see who would give up first—which I lost. I gave up many times while John hung on, grimly, refusing to quit. Since I couldn't leave him alone, I had to drift helplessly along with him.

Finally, six miles below camp, we heard a rapid. The rapid was insignificant, but the acre of driftwood below it was a gift from heaven. It was soon ablaze. We kept backing farther from the fire until we were about 150 yards away, each on his own boulder slowly turning, one side baked by 30 tons of blazing wood, the other freezing in the pelting rain.

No sooner were we afloat again than we began to plan the next warm-up break. We swam a few jolly little rapids and three or four miles downstream saw another huge pile of wood. By this time the wood was rather rain soaked, so our fire sent up a huge column of smoke. As we stood well back and watched the column rise into the vastness of the canyon, we realized how insignificant it was. The chances of anyone seeing the smoke were about zero, and we gave up any idea of using a fire, however large, as a distress signal. Better save the effort.

A glimmer of sun tantalized us back into the river, but no sooner were we swimming than the clouds returned from their hiding places behind the walls and poured rain down on us again. It felt like standing in a cold shower while someone threw buckets of ice water on us.

Back in the river we encountered a few smallish rapids which helped distract us from the cold for awhile. Forster Rapid had a mansion-sized rock in the middle which sent John swimming vigorously toward the side of the river. Two miles farther along we came to S-shaped Fossil Rapid. Neither of us negotiated it well, and we found ourselves grounded about halfway through. Just after Fossil the granite reappeared. While we knew we'd be able to find campsites in the granite, we also knew there would be no shelter from the rain. On top of the rising granite, however, were strata of sandstones and shales which were deeply undercut, leaving wide caves that promised perfect covered campsites. These strata were riding up on the granite, however, and would soon be out of reach. By the time we had agreed on a place, the lowest sheltered ledge was 100 feet off the water.

That was the night John was cleaning his pistol and dropped a vital little pin in the silt. He knew within inches where it had fallen, but before he was through he had raked our campsite with his fingers and his fork, had panned the area like a gold miner and finally, after dark, had cascaded cupful after cupful of silt through his flashlight beam hoping to spot the pin. The process consumed

"This River Is Out to Get Me"

a few drams of whiskey—maybe more than a few because the last thing I heard as I went to sleep was, "Pin's hiding . . . doesn't want me to find it . . . doesn't *want* me to have a pistol. It keeps moving, right now it's under this big pile of sand. Can't sit here and look for it, pile's too big. Go to sleep poor John. Go to bed. Poor-old-John-without-a-pistol-Daggett."

Our maps showed us we were 30 miles from Havasu Creek and the long climb to Havasu Village. From the first time we had heard of it, we had planned to stop at Havasu and visit the smallest Indian tribe in the U.S., Grand Canyon dwellers from prehistoric times. At one time we had considered resupplying completely there. Even after abandoning that idea as impractical, we still wanted to climb to the tiny, protected village just to see it. Now it was again becoming apparent that our huge consumption of food made supplementing our supplies there a wise idea. Also we could mail exposed film out.

The sun was up in the morning and the day promised to be another good one of shooting through the "granite." We tumbled through a half dozen rapids and between them drifted down some of the narrowest passages in the river. In these narrows there were no accommodating silt banks, no friendly piles of driftwood; this was the most remote part of the canyon with no trails on the plateau above, no early signs of man nearby.

The sun was bright and hot and reflected off the polished rock so intensely that we kept our eyes slitted. It was so hot we had to keep dashing water on the black rubber of our boxes to keep them from burning our bare forearms. The temperature in the airless side canyons must have risen to 130 degrees—the whole area had a dead, hell-like feeling. And yet the water of the river was as cold as ever. It was strange to be broiled on top and frozen below. At times we wished we could swim along upside down. At our one warm-up break that morning we couldn't stay out of the water long because we became intolerably hot in our black rubber shirts.

Shortly after the break we came to Bedrock Rapids. Even as we approached we could see this wasn't going to be easy. First the river bent left around the boulder fan of Bedrock Canyon, then it shot directly at Bedrock itself, a great rock island which split the flowing water as a whirling saw slices a log. Half the river was diverted sharply to the right, completing an S bend while the other half disappeared into unknown hazards behind Bedrock.

John, still fearful of all large rocks, hung back while I swam ahead. As I poured down the tongue, sizing up the problem as fast as I could, I saw no way to avoid hitting the rock island. The whole force of the river was dashing against it like surf pounding a cliff. Every few seconds the water rushed up the rock face then came back down again in a big curling wave which formed and broke and reformed again.

I was swimming furiously to the right side of the river, driving hard to try to keep away from the rock, when I saw that if I could catch that wave just right I might use it to push me off the rock. It was body surfing, pure and simple, but the timing had to be very good.

At what I thought was just the right moment I paused, going with the flow, and let the river hurl me at that rock with frightening force. I had guessed right — just as I was about to hit, the thousands of gallons of water that had gotten there first rushed back, carrying me with them. I came so close I could have kissed that big jagged red monster.

As I slid along its side, the river now carrying me parallel to the island, I saw a nasty little fishhook of rock at its downstream end. With a few extra strokes I was able to slip past it and turn to watch John.

John was playing it safe. He was much farther to the right than I had been. I lost him for a moment in the spray — then he reappeared right up against Bedrock. He was fending off the rock with his hands. I started for shore, swimming backwards so I could watch John. He was swept swiftly along the edge of the island. Then he got turned around backwards.

Suddenly he stopped. He had been going so fast and was stopped so abruptly that I could see, almost feel, the shudder that shook his body. The water poured over him and submerged him. He was rolled backwards for a few yards. I could see a swim fin or his head project crazily out of the water and then disappear in the brown.

Just past Bedrock he came up and stayed. By this time I was on a little patch of silt and stood up to see better. John was in a little whirlpool not moving. President Harding Rapid all over again? But this time there seemed to be no blood, and when he got out of the whirlpool and began to swim slowly toward me it was obvious he was furious.

As he got closer I heard him ranting and raving and saying bad things. When I could understand what he was saying I discovered that high on his list of targets was *me*.

As I helped him climb out on our little silt bank he moved very slowly, very painfully. Between groans he continued his expostulations.

"Damn you, Beer! You're the luckiest guy in the world. I was way to the right of you. When I saw you get by with no problem, I was sure I was safe. Then that goddam wave disappeared! It was there for you, but when I came along, no siree. No way is the Colorado going to make it easy for old John. All of a sudden the way was nice and clear and all downhill into that rock. No wave for old hit-the-rocks-John. I was pushing and shoving all along that rock. Right next to the son of a bitch!"

"Why did you turn around?"

"You don't think I wanted to, do you? I had just spotted that little hook when the river jerked me around backward and slammed me into it. Hard."

"Boy, I'll say. I could feel it from here."

"My back feels broken."

It looked that way from the way John was acting. He couldn't sit or stand erect. Every time he moved, he groaned a little. He had hit right on the base of his spine, driven by the full force of the river. Worse than the pain was his anger and frustration.

"I did all the intelligent planning. I watched you, Bill, and then figured I'd play it even safer. I did everything right but I was cheated! Robbed! It's like that damn rock reached out and grabbed me. You know, I think this river is out to get me. I mean it!"

"Hey, you could have broken a leg, or been killed."

That sobering thought seemed to mollify John somewhat, though he did carry on a bit on the theme that the rapids seemed to be getting worse and bigger and more dangerous the farther we went. It wasn't that he wanted to quit. John felt the Colorado River had hurled a personal challenge at him and he was determined to win.

In fact, he insisted on going on even though getting into the water was a slow agonizing operation for him. The water, however, gave him some support and the cold numbed the pain, so perhaps he was better off swimming than not. After a couple of fair-sized rapids—Deubendorff and Tapeats—we stopped for lunch at 135 Mile Rapid.

After lunch John took a few still photos of me swimming 135 Mile Rapid and then followed behind. He caught up in a section called Granite Narrows where the rocks close in on the river tightly; in places the river is less than 40 feet wide. It is a gloomy place. Just downstream from the narrows we came upon Deer Creek Falls, one of the Colorado River's more beautiful sights. Seeing this lovely waterfall dropping out of a dark slit in the cliff to plunge more than a hundred feet down through the sunlight, we had to stop. I doubt if any canyon traveler, past or future, ever passes up Deer Creek Falls.

It was at Deer Creek that I wasted five dollars of film taking movies of a bird swimming underwater. I thought it was a freak of evolution which had appeared in one of the Grand Canyon's micro-environments. Of course it wasn't—just an ordinary water ouzel. John thought I ought to pay him his half of the film cost when he found out.

"This River Is Out to Get Me"

We departed, regretting it was too early to camp, and swam downstream looking for the perfect rapid to photograph. We needed movies of one of us going through a typical rapid to illustrate what we did a dozen times a day. We wanted a rapid with a curve, a high, sloping bank for camera positions and a convenient eddy at the bottom to help the swimmer get out of the current. We planned to take multiple runs of one rapid.

We found our ideal rapid at Fishtail. It was really too early to stop, but a look at the map consoled us. Even with our late start and early finish we had logged 14 miles, and though this wasn't our best mileage to date, we had fallen farther, 135 feet, than on any other day's run. At 139$^{1/2}$ miles we were halfway to my car at Pierce Ferry. I commented, "Halfway, John old pal, it's all downhill from here on."

John, gently exploring the lump on his tailbone groused, "Yeah, like Hell is downhill from here."

Our campsite was only a few feet off the water, but we did have a spring trickling out of the cliff nearby and both enjoyed clear water showers; it was nice to get all the silt out of our hair, beards and underwear. We were cramped by the talus slopes and John found the only level spot on the sand a foot off the water; I chose to dig a ledge out of the talus slope for my sleeping bag. John got clever and, before he went to bed, marched a line of little sticks standing up in the sand from his bed to the water. By counting them, he could tell if the river were rising. We were sure it was, as we had an unusual amount of driftwood floating with us today.

That night the never quiet Colorado with its rapids and whirlpools and bubbling boils was noisier than ever with the *schluurp, schlump* of sandbanks giving way to the rising water. John's stick system worked well. Every hour or so I was awakened by the beam of his flashlight as he counted stakes. There were always one or two fewer. At last count I saw only two.

But we were both too tired to keep it up. At dawn I was awakened by John grumbling below me. I looked down to see almost all our campsite under water and John's sleeping bag half in the river.

John relaxes in warm sunshine.

"This River Is Out to Get Me"

"Now I *know* the river is out to get me," he announced. "Well, I've had my warnings and I'm going to be *really* careful from now on."

That morning we cooked on a boulder. The river had risen by this date to about 15,000 cubic feet per second, and there was no sand left.

After breakfast I unloaded my boxes and repacked them with lighter driftwood, and we climbed to the head of the rapids. After some surveying and discussing, we thought we could get the film footage we needed in four runs. Because of John's painful back, the original plan to split chores had to change. I got to do all the swimming while he sat on a rock and took pictures.

After each swim through the rapid I had to get ashore, put on sneakers, put my boxes on my back and hike along the cliffs for half a mile. After each trip in the hot sun wearing a rubber shirt, sweatshirt and woolen underwear, the cold Colorado was a delight. I made the four runs while John sat dozing on a rock, trying to make it look like a great effort when he moved to a new camera site. It was well after noon when we started downriver again.

We took only one warm-up break that afternoon, but when we came to Upset Rapid it looked so ideal for movies that we again stopped to film. This time, back or no back, it was Daggett's turn to swim. I set up and waited interminably for him, sure the sun would set before he arrived. And when he did come around the bend into the rapids, I thought he was struggling unnecessarily much just for the camera. "Ham" was the word that stuck in my mind.

He disappeared into the shadows and I set about making camp. He was a long time returning. About two hours in fact, and well after dark. He explained that he had discovered he was going through the rapids with an overly friendly railroad tie and that by the time he got free of his dangerous companion he had missed all the good whirlpools and had landed about a mile downstream. There was no way back along shore so he had to do some swimming and some rock climbing. It was my turn to have the hot soup ready.

150 Mile Canyon, which gave birth to Upset Rapid, is another of the delights of the Grand Canyon. It's more of a corridor than a canyon. We walked into it a few hundred yards and, while its walls rose vertically four hundred feet, we could still touch both sides with outstretched arms. It seemed no wider at the top than the bottom and so narrow that the sun never reached most parts of it. At the mouth the bottom widened out so that we were camped in a virtual cave. On one side was a high silt bank with a level floor which gave us a wonderful overlook of Upset Rapid and the canyon in both directions. All in all, a perfect spot. Except in a flash flood. Happily, the skies were clear that night and even though a flash flood could be produced by a storm many miles away, we felt confident we were safe.

We were both feeling pain that night. John still couldn't sit or lie on his back—it was either stand or lie face down—and his finger was still useless. My usual collection of nicks and bruises seemed to have concentrated in my feet, which were so swollen and sore that I walked with a hobble. The climb to Havasu the next day began to look like an ordeal.

In the morning we were again faced with getting into Upset Rapid from too close to the brink. I made it narrowly, but John lost his boxes and got sorely smacked while chasing them through the rapid. Even so, it was a great rapid and an exhilarating way to start the day! We were in the water, through the heaving, turbulent rapids and around the bend before we caught our breath.

We were less than an hour swimming to the mouth of Havasu Canyon. It's a tricky entrance with little clue to tell you it's coming. The cliffs descend into the water so there was no chance to get out and survey the problem. I was slightly ahead of John and hugging the left side of the river so as not to miss the entrance. With no warning I went around a projection of rock and there it was! Bright blue water and hard swimming upstream against the current of Havasu Creek. I yelled back at John, "Wait till you see this!"

He hurried to join me but didn't hug the cliff as closely as I did. As he came around the corner I saw his astonished look as he saw the beautiful Havasu, then the even more astonished look as he was swept away toward Havasu Rapid. John is a powerful swimmer, but that morning he exceeded himself. It appeared he had an outboard motor he kicked his feet so hard. Pushing his boxes like a river tugboat he plowed his way up against both the Colorado and the Havasu and swam into the blue tunnel that is the mouth of this stream.

The creek joins the river through a thin cleft with overhanging walls. The walls and creek bottom are white with limestone deposits, and the water is a startling aquamarine. The bright sun shining into one end of this tunnel was caught and reflected a thousand times until even the air seemed colored blue. After the brown, harsh Colorado, we couldn't believe this. After a hundred feet or so of hard upstream swimming in strangely warm water we came to a place where we could climb out on the rock.

We made packs of our sleeping bags, enclosing exposed film and a little food, and set off up Havasu Canyon, another of the delights of the Grand Canyon.

It would be about 12 miles to the village, the first nine of which had no trail. This lower part of Havasu Canyon was totally enchanting. A narrow 2,000-foot-deep canyon more than half formed by the smooth vertical Red Wall, its red walls were capped by the blue sky and floored with the most amazing series of bright blue pools separated by little white waterfalls and fringed with green trees and shrubs. The creek was lined with white lime deposits which gave it the appearance of a series of suburban swimming pools climbing in steps up the canyon. We couldn't get over it.

With no trail, the going was difficult. At times we inched along the cliffs, sometimes waded upstream, sometimes stumbled through thickets, often backtracking. About halfway up we began to see a few footprints, then we came upon a pile of discarded rusty tin cans. What a shock! It was the first litter we had seen since Lees Ferry. But from there up to the village we saw more and more litter, cigarette butts, gum wrappers, etc. It made us both appreciate where we had been.

Neither of us was walking very well; we both had acutely sore feet and realized we had acquired more injuries in the river than we had thought. Now that we were using our feet for walking — our bodies no longer both supported and anesthetized by cold water — the injuries showed up. From the river to the village is 12 miles, but we moved so slowly that darkness caught us just as we reached Mooney Falls, less than seven miles up the canyon from the Colorado. We made barely one mile per hour.

Facing us was a 300-foot cliff extending across the canyon from wall to wall — but not your ordinary cliff. It appeared to be made of fountains of frozen stone, as if fan-shaped jets of liquid rock had shot out from a hundred places on the face of the cliff and just as they curved down had instantly congealed. Each of these curved fans seemed to drip scores of stone icicles, which festooned the face of the cliff with a thousand vertical streamers. In the center of these solid brown streamers fell the shimmering 230-foot white ribbon of Mooney Falls, plunging into a marvelous half-acre blue pool.

We were speechless. The whole place was a fairy tale scene.

It was the litter that told us we could somehow get up this cliff with all its overhangs and stalagtites. But we were darned if we could figure out how. The bats came out in droves from the cliff. We thought better of trying to do any tricky rock climbing in the dark. So we just camped there at the foot of Mooney.

The next morning we discovered a well-built trail cut up through the cliff using tunnels here and there and offering viewing openings complete with steel guard rails. And at the top of the falls the trail became well-trampled.

A little way above the falls, hobbling worse than ever now, we came upon campers having breakfast outside some old prospectors' cabins. This group of people were being shepherded by a professional guide who charged them for this taste of outdoor living. John muttered, "Pretty good way to run a hotel. No hotel, no beds, no food, and the guests do all the chores." And then with a laugh we realized that these people, whom we regarded as civilization with tents and cots and all the comforts, were themselves sure they were out in the wilderness. We were a little startled when they almost immediately guessed who we were and began with a flood of questions. I hustled us away, only to have John grouse that if we'd lingered we could have wrangled breakfast.

We passed the next two waterfalls in Havasu's series of three — both lovely, but neither as spectacular as Mooney — and arrived at the village. We would have walked right through it but for the church, a large stone-faced Quonset hut with a bell tower on one side. Under the roof was a big loudspeaker — to carry the word to any reluctant churchgoers who decided to sleep late on Sundays. This had to be the center of town.

Nearby was a flagpole with a U.S. flag. There were a couple of horses tied to the fence and some little boys swinging on the gate. Behind the flagpole was a nondescript building with several crude signs on it. "Havasupai Sub Agency — Supai, Arizona" and "Havasu Tourist Enterprise Office, Register Here" were on one door; on the other we read, "Post Office — Supai, Arizona" and "BASKETS FOR SALE."

On the steps lounged a couple of Red Men. They began the pow wow.

"Hey, you guys them Frog Men?"

"Uh . . . yeah. Say, could you tell . . . "

"You guys didn't really swim down that river, did you?"

"Uh . . . yeah. Say, could you tell . . . "

"Who you guys kiddin'? Nobody's that crazy. Not even White Men."

"Uh . . . sure. Say, could you tell us where the Post Office is?"

At that moment a little white man with thinning hair came around the corner carrying a hoe. With the hoe he pointed to the sign in front of the door that read "Post Office—Supai, Arizona." We went in and at once faced the world's widest woman.

Her beam was not less than one yard. A perfect 36 inches across the shoulders and hips with proportionate face and feet. Havasupai are wide people, but this lady must have been mother-of-them-all. Her English was mostly mumbles and sibilants delivered with her hand covering her mouth, and only when the wife of The Indian Agent showed up were we able to understand how to get our mail entrusted to the care of the Federal Government. At that it took an hour. Starving by now, we asked about The Store. The Postmistress managed to communicate that it was next door. We went next door. Pretty soon The Postmistress lumbered over. She was The Storekeeper.

There were several holes in the floor, at least one of which we were told was caused when the floor gave way under The Storekeeper the year before. Goods were piled on the floor or in boxes scattered about. We spent every last cent we had on food. Once outside we wondered if we'd have to squat in Supai's main street to cook breakfast. Fortunately, we were directed to The Guest House, which had been The Hospital till The Medicine Man had it shut down.

Just as we finished our gargantuan breakfast the man with the hoe strolled in.

"Howdy," was our official greeting from The Indian Agent.

"Howdy, howdy," we replied, hoping to open things up a bit.

Silence.

"You fellows them Frog Men?"

We confessed.

"There's a few people been callin' you. Want you to call back. Don't know if the phone works today, though."

We strolled over to The Telephone, which was next door in The Indian Agent's living room. John attempted our calls with much shouting and repeating—the telephone worked only intermittently that day.

He informed the Park Service of our progress and timetable. He learned that our movies, mailed from Grand Canyon Village, had indeed been fine—were excellent in fact—and that excerpts, especially John swimming Soap Creek Rapid and me in Hance, had been shown on TV all over the country. Another spate of news stories had come out, including interviews with Park officials and others—even the honeymoon couple who had given me the lift. Now that we had reached Supai there would be a few more news stories. Publicity was of no concern to us—we felt so cut off from the world that it was as if the uproar were happening to someone else—but the news about the camera working was wonderful.

We should have left then to return to our river, but our feet were so sore and swollen and so cut up that we thought it wise to give them a rest. Besides, we were enjoying Supai and its people. We spent the day getting to know some of the residents and learning some of their fascinating history. We were treated by the Havasupai as part supernatural, part crazy. They held the Colorado River in superstitious awe. They warned us of the dangers of Lava Falls, 25 miles downriver, though none of them had ever seen the rapid.

In the morning our feet were no better; my own dainty size thirteens looked like stuffed sausages with toes. Oh well, it was all downhill. About halfway down to the Colorado an old ankle injury of John's acted up and he limped badly. Both of us fell into the creek more than once—in my case scrambling a dozen fresh eggs in my sleeping bag. We arrived at dusk and camped at the mouth of Havasu Canyon, sure in the knowledge that swimming rapids and fighting whirlpools was easier than climbing up and down Havasu Canyon in tattered tennis shoes.

8

Lava Falls and Burro Meat

The next morning was our nineteenth day since leaving Lees Ferry, and a splendid day it was. After breakfast it was a delight to go swimming in warm water for a change. The warmth lasted only two or three minutes and then we were shoved out of the glowing blue tunnel of Havasu into the cold, brown Colorado and whisked down Havasu Rapid.

We took only short breaks—just enough to drive the cold out of our bones—by rolling back and forth in the hot sand. No fires for us this day. We were relaxed and confident, swimming a rapid about every mile—none of them offering any real challenge, just fun. John even took a nap on one break.

This was the narrowest part of the Grand Canyon, the only place where you can shout from rim to rim—that is, if your voice will carry two to three miles. The North Rim appeared to be almost straight up over our heads, 5,000 feet above us.

Camping time was again signaled to us by one of nature's clocks. With thousands of limestone caves to choose from, it's not surprising that tens of millions of bats live in the Grand Canyon. As soon as we saw what we called the "bourgeois" bats, we knew it was time to stop. These were the ordinary bats that came out in great hordes just before dark. We gave pet names to two other classes of bats: the "misfits" and the "gluttons." The gluttons stayed out gorging themselves until well after everybody else had gone home. But our favorites were the poor misfits, who just couldn't adjust themselves to the routines of bat society. They stayed out all day wandering around in the blinding light, scavenging what bugs they could.

We camped that night opposite Lava Pinnacle, one of the landmarks of the river. It's a chunk of black lava as big as a three-story building and looks like the end of a large Tootsie Roll jutting out of the water. Our map showed us that we had made 21 miles that day—our best so far—and we had swum through 18 rapids, none of which were of any consequence on the Colorado though they would have been major rapids on many other rivers.

We were again in high spirits. Lava Falls would be tomorrow, but tonight we were undaunted by any upcoming problems. We were both unable to walk much and mostly crawled around camp, but even that seemed trivial. After all, we could still swim. In the event of a broken leg or other injury, we knew there was no climbing out of the canyons in our condition so there would be no choice but to splint the leg, make a raft of our rubber boxes and driftwood, and carry on down river.

We had a little celebration that night for another reason. It was my 26th birthday. John dug out a beautiful canned ham he had hidden for the occasion; I made biscuits and we gorged ourselves on the best goodies from each store of supplies. John even had a present for me: a jackknife he had been keeping as a birthday present. When he was buying it in L.A. he said he knew that it would be a great celebration when he gave it to me. If for no other reason than that we would both still be alive.

The next morning we were up and down at the river early. We were eager to tackle Lava Falls, to take on the worst the Colorado River had to offer. But, the cold water again dampened our enthusiasm and we discovered an immediate need to make some more movies. The banks were nice and muddy here and it seemed a great place to do a "quicksand" sequence. John, of course, was chosen for the role of the hapless victim of the slimy mud while I got to be the clean, dry cameraman. This took a good couple of hours, at the end of which time we were heated up enough to go swimming.

It was a short drift down to Lava Falls. Even when we first heard it from a mile upstream, we knew we were facing something different. The voice of Lava Falls was deeper and seemed more ominous than that of other rapids. It chewed and growled in an angry basso and from a half mile upstream we could look down toward this uproar and see jets of water spitting into the air.

A little apprehensive, we pulled into the right bank a quarter mile above the brink, a good deal farther upstream than was our custom. Taking the movie camera we began a painful and slow climb along the hot black lava and sharp rocks. We couldn't see more than a corner of Lava Falls until we were almost on top of it. When we finally climbed up the last forty-foot chunk of lava and stood looking down on the rapid, we were dumbfounded. At first sight, Lava Falls seemed to deserve its ugly reputation.

On second sight, it still deserved it. We had never seen such an angry, snarling maelstrom. Half-way through the tumult, a black rock jutted out toward the center of the rapid. I climbed down to it while John made movies of me surveying the rapid. Then he joined me and we stood together on the rock in the rapid while the water leaped up trying to wash us off. We were near the middle of the clamor and had to shout in each other's ear to be heard.

"How does it look to you from here?"

"Worse!"
"Think there's a chance, Bill?"
"What?"
"I say, do you think there's a chance we can swim it?"
"No."

Talking was difficult; we silently stared at the rapid. Then I took the camera and shot some footage of the boiling water. Through the tiny hole of the viewfinder there was room only for brown waves and spray, and I wondered if I weren't wasting film.

What a place! Four thousand feet above the rapid the volcano Vulcan's Throne poises on the North Rim. Not long ago in geologic terms this volcano poured liquid streams of lava into the Colorado, damming up the river for miles in a boiling, fuming lake. A few eons later, the Colorado had cut its way back down through the lava, leaving little sign of its great dam except Lava Falls. Prospect Canyon, coming in here from the south, had shoved its boulders into the river, nearly joining the lava that had poured down the north wall, damming up the Colorado and resulting in a vicious frothing rapid. The water whips and churns violently and the rocks all seem to have been whetted sharp—just for us.

From the north side where we stood, fingers of lava pointed out toward midstream. The one we stood on lifted a knuckle above the tormented surface like the crooked finger of a giant's hand. The others lay beneath the water, revealed from time to time by the great curling waves and holes they created. Each of these lava ridges was guarded by a wave that constantly rolled upstream, ready to pound any bit of flotsam that came its way. From the other bank, well out toward the middle of the stream, rocks broke to the surface like hobnails on a boot.

The currents were a maze obscured by the spray. Standing on the giant's finger near the center of Lava Falls, I tried to watch hunks of driftwood tumbling through, but the water was so frothy that the only ones I saw were those that were hurled onto the rock at our feet. The water rushed by at nearly 30 miles per hour. The whole thing looked hopeless.

There was almost no tongue to this rapid. Instead there was a brink. Like water pouring over a wall, Lava Falls started with an abrupt drop; the rest of the way was just pure confusion. In all, the rapid dropped 37 feet. There appeared to be one narrow break in the wall but it was too close to the north side. If we came that way we were sure to be slammed against one of the fingers of lava. The only normal thing about this rapid was that it did stream out into a long tail, flanked by the usual whirlpools. No wonder it was regarded as the worst rapid on the river, the standard by which all others were measured.

The only possible course was to come through that break, but since no swimmer had enough power to avoid the lava, somehow or other we'd have to bounce off it. Or maybe we would be dragged across one or two or three ridges of lava before being bashed into the last. It would be something like Bedrock, where we'd needed to catch the wave just right. Except that here there were several waves in succession that needed to be caught. There were about 14,000 cubic feet of water *per second* pouring over that lava very fast and we were both thinking how helpless we would be once we ventured into this rapid.

John didn't like the rocks. He was willing to let me take the lead here and would do whatever I did. I was not at all sure I was going to swim through *this* rapid. I worked my way back toward our first vantage point. I wished that I had taken the trouble to open a box and get out my sneakers—the lava was very sharp and very hot and there were thorny cacti about. I also wished I had a pair of gloves.

I reached a little knot of driftwood just above one of the big breaking waves and tossed a chunk of wood into the spume.

Lost.

I threw in a bigger piece.

Gone.

I found a log I could barely lift and slung it out. I caught one or two glimpses of it as it swirled through the waves and passed John. Well, at least it didn't get jammed up against a rock. I tried another log, but barely saw it after it hit the water.

No sense standing here throwing wood in the river all day.

I climbed higher for a different perspective.

Down by the water with the camera, John was thinking all the while that I would give it up, but the more I watched the rapid, the less dangerous it seemed. Familiarity breeding contempt? I chose what looked like the best course for a swimmer and then compared it with a couple of alternatives. I imagined myself in the water and mentally followed myself through the rapids.

It was horrible.

But after I swam it 10 or 15 times in my mind the whole process began to seem more like a dream than reality.

Oh, why not?

A little hypnotized, I saw myself signaling John that I was going to swim through, and started working my way upstream. All the while I kept my mind busy with little details of the course, estimates of current speeds and direction. I looked for a guidepost so I would enter at the optimum spot. Of course from six inches off the water it would all look different, and a few feet one way or another were important—vital actually.

Down at the river's edge, where I couldn't see any of the rapid, I caught sight of a persistent little spout of water that kept shooting higher than the brink in the same spot every few seconds. I felt sure it would guide me.

Fear began to take hold of me. It was the strangest feeling; I was so scared there wasn't room for any other emotion, and hardly room for any thoughts. At this point I had swum through some hundred plus rapids. This was just one more, I tried to tell myself. But I wasn't convincing; I really had found no safe way through the rapid; it was going to be a matter of trusting to luck. Not my nature.

Much sooner than I wanted to, I found myself back at my

boxes. It seemed so much quieter here; the river slid by me smooth and oily, the roar of Lava Falls now somewhat muted. I stood hesitating for long moments, like a kid about to jump off a high wall. "Ready? Here I come. One . . . two . . . three . . . "

Couldn't jump. Bladder too full.

That taken care of, my body demanded further attention.

"You can't go swimming now," it said. "I'm hungry."

So the condemned man sat down to lunch.

Down on the lava by the Falls, John was alone with the camera and his thoughts as I had been way back at Soap Creek Rapid. He cautioned himself to keep on filming as long as there was nothing else he could do to help me and then to be sure not to drop the camera in the water if he had to go after me, but to lay it down carefully so he could return for it if possible. From his rock downstream the rapid posed little threat; he could even dive in the water from where he stood. It seemed like I had been away for a week. It was probably about an hour. He got bored waiting for me. And hungry.

Back upstream I finished my lunch and strapped my boxes up tightly. With no further diversions available I waded toward deep water and the current. As I lowered my chest into the water between my boxes I tried to give our customary howl at the cold, but my tightened throat only permitted a peep.

As I drifted toward the brink and the unseen rapid I tried to prepare somehow, swim around or something, like a fighter shadow boxing and dancing around the ring before a bout. And I played a little game, estimating every few moments whether I could still chicken out and reach shore. When I passed the point where nothing was possible but to swim Lava Falls, I relaxed. There were no more decisions to make. In peace I studied the cliffs, the water, a piece of driftwood or two floating along with me and chuckled at myself for being there. The roar came closer. Thirty or forty feet from the brink I sought my little water spout.

It wasn't to be seen.

Portrait of a swimmer's two precious rubber boxes resting in the silt

Lava Falls and Burro Meat

I rushed toward the rapid without any idea of whether I was where I was supposed to be. Way downstream I could see the big rock and little John sitting on top taking movies. I levered myself higher on the boxes to see the rapid—to get oriented.

It was too late. I was 20 feet too far left and was going to drop over the worst brink of the rapid. I slipped backwards from my boxes stretching them out in front of me as far as I could, clinging to the straps with a madman's clutch. The current grabbed my boxes and sucked them downward with a yank that nearly pulled my arms out of their sockets. I plummeted down after them, and when they reached bottom and stopped momentarily, my face was jammed into them and my feet were flung over my head in an unwilling somersault.

The river grabbed my boxes and jerked them downstream again and I spun after them like the tail of a kite. We, my heavy boxes and I, were rolled and whipped somewhere in the mad mass of spray and rocks between the bottom and the roiled surface. It was dark underwater in that muddy river and I couldn't see where I was, where I was going or even which way was up. All I could do was hang on to my gyrating equipment in a violent crack-the-whip game. The river I thought I knew so well, that I thought I had mastered, was suddenly an angry giant pummeling and twisting me. It was trying to drown me in dark violence.

For a quick moment I was flung to the surface. It was a surprise to see daylight. I grabbed a lucky lung full of air and was plunged into the blackness again. I was rolled sideways, I was rolled end for end, my arms were jerked out then in, my legs were pumping frantically but for no good reason. I hit a couple of things, the bottom, maybe—scary enough, but trivial in light of what I knew was coming.

I wondered how I would hit the lava. With an arm, a leg, my back? Hopefully my boxes, still thrust out at arm's length when possible, would hit first.

I popped to the surface a second time. I was three feet from the lava knuckle and there was John sitting on top winding the camera!

"Why isn't he taking pictures? Here I am, nearly dead, about to be hurled at his feet and he's sitting on his duff."

Then a lucky surge threw me sideways, submerging me again, and I flew past the lava barely flicking it with my foot. Back on the surface, and on it to stay, I bounded on into the tail of the rapid. Wild with exuberance, I screamed triumph to the cliffs and swam for shore as hard as I could. When I reached shore the reaction set in; I was weak and motionless as the fear and excitement drained away with most of my strength.

I had, in understandable confusion, landed on the opposite shore. There was no way to communicate to John except by signals. I wanted to give him some idea of the safest channel. But I only confused him. One garbled set of signals included a slitting of the throat motion, and he understandably thought I was telling him it was too dangerous to try.

So John was confused, too. He had seen me swim Lava Falls. Or at least he had seen the beginning and the end since I was underwater for about three quarters of the run. And I was obviously safe and sound, so how could I be telling him to give it up? That wasn't our custom; if there was a decent chance we would take it, and if I'd gotten through, there was obviously a good chance John would too. So regardless of what nonsense I was trying to communicate from the other bank, John was going to go ahead and swim Lava Falls. But my little pantomime had him worried.

I watched John go through the same process I had. He stopped and looked at the water from every vantage point and threw in chunks of driftwood and paused for long spells just looking. Then he passed out of sight upstream.

I took my cheap little 35mm camera and hopped from boulder to boulder out into the rapid as far as I could, stationed myself on a slippery rock and waited while the dancing spray tried to soak my camera.

He wasn't long in coming.

I first saw John as a little yellow life jacket drifting downstream between two black rubber boxes. As he gathered speed I began clicking off pictures, the first one above the brink, then another as he plunged down through the break I had planned to follow. He was lost in the spray in the next picture, then he came to the surface too close to the right bank just upstream from that last block of lava. I took another picture. He was surely going to hit.

Then John showed he had learned his lessons—Harding and Bedrock, and the others—he rode the curling wave guarding the lava knuckle up into the wave and back down again, catching the edge and surfing neatly away from danger. He could have been at the beach. I took one more picture as he bounced through the tail.

He had run the rapid perfectly! I had goofed and was punished for my mistake, but John had been flawless. I was sure his confidence would be totally restored.

When I got back downstream to him he was indeed happy and smug, even suggesting we go back and swim Lava Falls again to get more movies. I offered to be cameraman.

He reconsidered and ate his lunch.

We agreed there was no doubt Lava Falls was the most difficult rapid of them all, but we weren't really sure we had done anything like "risk our lives." There was no doubt we'd do it again if the occasion arose, the next time with far less hesitation.

We jumped back into the water and swam downstream another three miles and called it quits for the day. We had only swum four miles that day, our worst mileage of the trip. But we had swum Lava Falls!

After Lava Falls the Colorado River lost its fearfulness. We still had a hundred miles to swim and didn't expect an easy time, but three weeks of training had honed our skills to the point that we could relax and enjoy the passing scene.

We were in a lonely part of the canyon. The nearby walls dropped low and the rim receded, leaving a vast valley of canyons and buttes where men were infrequent. We saw more wildlife here than on any other part of the river. Drifting silently, too far apart to talk as we often did, we were able to run up onto the animals without their being aware of us. To them we must have been just more driftwood floating down the river.

We saw the first set of beaver sitting in the mouths of caves they had dug into a steep bank. When they realized we were living creatures they disappeared, plop, plop, into the water. Later we saw more beaver and a ring-tailed civet, a rather rare cat.

The open country gave us a wide shallow river with gravel islands and rocky rapids. We always seemed to choose the wrong side of the islands and got pummeled for doing so. Then the wind came up to remind us of earlier miserable days. We had almost forgotten what it was like to swim with icy spray stinging our faces and sand blinding us. We kept on as long as we could, but when we saw a nice wooded area tucked into a ravine at about Mile 197 we called it quits again, trading a few more miles for a sheltered night. It was indeed pleasant that night to look out from our protected little snarl, to hear the wind howl, to see spray and sand and leaves zip by and know that we weren't going to spend the evening fighting flying sparks, nor wake up in the morning covered with sand and ashes.

That evening I was attacked by a craving for sweets. A big starchy dinner didn't help; after I finished I started in on my stock of candy bars. Already most of my sugar and honey had vanished, and on this night I ate every last one of my remaining candy bars — well over a dozen — and *still* wanted more. Even though we had added all we could afford to our stock while at Supai, we wondered if we were going to have enough food to get us through the remaining 82 miles. We had swum 15 miles this day and needed to do as well or better every remaining day. Or go hungry.

The next morning dawned as one of our lousiest. The wind was howling, the sky overcast, and we were treated to intermittent rain. It was a shabby day and we were struck by the shabbiness surrounding us. The trees and brush were tattered by the wind, our river clothes were muddy, ripped, patched and stained. All our equipment was dirty, worn and banged up, looking like it had been salvaged from some dump.

Silently we returned to the cold river and swam downstream into another day of shade and shallow rapids. We grimly clipped off five miles and as many rapids before stopping to light a pile of driftwood and then plunging back in. We planned to stop again after another five miles at Granite Park. Just before we stopped John found himself in a rapid caroming along the cliff that formed its bank, fending off the cliff with hands and feet as he was spun round and round down the river. He was dizzy when he finished, but successful at not getting hurt.

Shortly after our break we saw a small family of burros grazing on the talus slope. John was well downstream of me, but we evidently had the same thought as we both pulled ashore. Burro steaks.

It would be an interesting experiment in eating and would stretch our food supply. And if it was good, we could carry some meat along with us. Anyway, it was a lousy day for swimming.

I got out my 22 pistol, now a little rusty and, barefooted, snuck up on the little band. We felt little concern about killing one of these gentle beasts; we knew the serious problems they were causing in the canyons. Descendants of pack animals abandoned by prospectors, they had multiplied rapidly and were beginning to drive out species native to the area and to denude much of the sparse vegetation. They had even occasionally startled some of the pack mules carrying precious cargoes of tourists on the Bright Angel Trail. Burro-extermination expeditions had been undertaken by Park Service and other government agencies with only limited success.*

So it was with a clear conscience that I took aim on a young-

---

*Later, these efforts to save the big horn sheep, deer and other native species from starvation became very controversial and were ultimately frustrated by animal lovers, who thus favored the survival of the intruder species . . . and provoked the exasperation of the Park Service.

looking male burro. But my conscience was the only asset I had. The pistol was gritty and rusty and given to jamming, and I was shivering and my teeth were chattering from the cold river and still drizzling rain. But I knew I had hit him. I could actually hear the little bullet hit his flank. The other four burros turned and looked at me. My target quivered his flank as if to drive off a fly and turned to look at me too. I fired again, and again. This time my shots had somewhat more effect.

All five burros began to amble away from my noisy pistol.

I stalked them relentlessly. I fired more shots. I fired a whole clip of bullets. Some of these missed because I saw the little puffs of dirt where they hit. But most were hits. I reloaded and fired another clip. Finally when I had shot half a box of ammunition I stood up out of my hunter's crouch and cursed them soundly. This annoyed them and they strolled up the little draw that cut through the cliffs. I turned back toward the river.

I met John coming up. He had his shoes on and carried his knife, ready to dress out the kill.

"Where is he, Bill?"

"Where is who?" I innocently asked.

"Our dinner for tonight, of course."

"Aw, I hit that durned animal but he didn't seem to notice it. This gun is useless."

John wanted to give me his shoes so I could continue the chase, but instead I handed him the gun and said, "It's all your show."

I don't fancy myself a hunter. I have never killed a thing. But it was humiliating to be so defeated by my first wild beast—and a jackass at that.

We spent the next half-hour trying to outflank the burro band, John running across terraces, scrambling up cliffs and down draws, all the while signaling orders to me. Barefooted, I got pretty far out of the picture, but John proved he didn't need help. He outran and outflanked the burros twice, getting in good shots both times. He finally drove our target to his knees and was about to administer the good old coup de grace when the good old pistol jammed.

John, always on the offensive, picked up a large rock, charged the band, scattering all but the wounded quarry, and proceeded to kill our dinner with the rock. He cut off a hind quarter and we headed down to camp where we built a fire and began the preparation of delicious burro steaks.

Actually, burro steaks aren't really delicious. They're sort of nauseating. John declared we would eat only prime filet, but neither of us realized that those choice cuts had been left up on the talus slope; what we had were flank steaks. They were only slightly tough and tasted only a little fishy. John made a full meal of barbecued burro, washed down with whiskey. Grizzled and dirty, he was out of the Old West. Queasy Bill turned to canned macaroni.

We did agree, though, that we needn't take any burro meat along with us.

Despite our feeling that things were getting easier for us, we continued to be subjected to incessant erosion. This night we were impressed with how closely our hands and feet resembled turkey claws. Withered and scaly, they were bleeding at the joints and under the nails. The burro chase had aggravated our sore feet. We were again forced to mostly crawl around camp.

The next morning we both ripped into our food supply like freed prisoners. We teased each other about looking and acting as if we'd just gotten out of a concentration camp, and wolfed down nearly half our remaining breakfast supplies, then collapsed on the sand till nearly noon. With the late start we couldn't stop often, so we took just two breaks that day. It was a day of small rapids and big whirlpools and the miles came hard. At lunch I was down to a small snack and had to watch John as he greedily ate all his candy, dried fruit, cookies and whatever else he had left. I was hungry, but at least we were both now even – out of lunches. Our boxes had begun to empty because of the film we'd mailed out, all the food we'd eaten, and all the clothing that had been destroyed. We had begun to pack them with driftwood to help keep their shape; this way they were also no longer so heavy.

John was happily digesting his lunch when we heard a little *slurp*. A normal sort of slurp that we often heard when banks were caving in. This time I stood up and looked. One pair of our boxes had ridden down with the silt and was floating away in the river. I started to the rescue when I saw they were John's boxes. So I sat down. Him and his big lunch. I was tempted to say nothing, but after a pause, announced,

"Say John."

"Yeah?"

"Uh, I think your boxes just left."

"What!" He leaped to his feet, grabbed his fins and dove in. The boxes were almost at midstream, about to tumble down a rapid. He barely caught them in time to shoot the rapid with them. I followed with a grin.

We pushed on, spurred by diminishing food supplies, and actually made our day's goal, Diamond Creek. We arrived late and were frozen stiff. Diamond Creek had made a huge delta and all over it were signs of people. Boards, nails, remnants of iron stoves and other paraphenalia still remained from the camp built in the mid 1920s for the first Grand Canyon damsite exploration. Boulder Canyon proved a better site, fortunately. A mile or so up Diamond Creek the first attempt at a Grand Canyon hotel had been built in 1884 and a stage road ran from the Colorado River up past the hotel to the nearest town on the railroad, Peach Springs. It is still the only road to reach the bottom of the Grand Canyon.

Using pieces of old stoves and junk, we set up a luxurious camp. With an unlimited supply of clear water nearby we even did some laundry. We boasted that we were so adapted to our river life now that given 30 dollars of groceries and new long johns every month, we could spend years swimming through the Grand Canyon.

9
Lost . . . and Found!

We were back in the "granite" again. The Lower Granite Gorge was not as dramatic as the first two; the hard rocks appear and disappear sporadically. But this did mean a narrower slot with bigger rapids and fewer rocky shallows. In one of these John thought he hit a rock. He felt a sharp blow to his back followed by a moist feeling spreading out from the point of impact. He was sure he had suffered a serious wound, but the cold deadened sensation. Then the cold grew intense. Finally he realized that he had been hit by a log in a rapid and it had torn a hole in his rubber shirt. From then on John complained bitterly as the icy waters of the Colorado poured in next to his skin. I was unsympathetic. Mine had never sealed itself properly and I had been perpetually wet from the first day.

The colors in this part of the Grand Canyon are more varied, irregular and vivid. The "granite" is shot through with seams and pockets of minerals of every shade. There are even flowers perched here and there among the rocks. Caves of every size abound in the limestone, and the same water action that has hollowed out the caves has redeposited the limestone in wonderful travertine formations up and down the walls. Sometimes we would see a little grouping of outdoor stalagmites sticking up only a few inches; in other places the formations were gigantic. At Mile 230 we passed Travertine Falls, a smooth flow of limestone that tapered up hundreds of feet like a buttress trying to hold up the mighty cliffs.

At 231 Mile Rapid we stopped to take movies—just one run of me going through because we wanted to get to Separation Rapid that night to make more movies of our swimming it in the morning. That was the dramatic place where three of Major Powell's first party separated, only to be murdered when they reached the rim.

We had one more unplanned stop that day when a group of cabins caught our attention. At first we thought it was a mining camp, but soon realized it was another dam survey site, this time for a proposed dam at Bridge Canyon which, like the one proposed at Diamond Creek, would have filled a good part of the Grand Canyon. In the old mess hall we found, amazingly enough, a fourteen-year-old jar of dried-up honey which we later dissolved and used on pancakes. I found an old cigarette and smoked it, to John's great disgust. After about an hour we pushed on to Separation Rapid.

We never found it.

We drifted for miles in a completely tame Colorado River. Not only was there no Separation Rapid, there were no rapids at all. We couldn't understand it; no one had told us about this. Never before had the river gone more than a couple of miles without rapids. It was nearly dark when we swam ashore, confused.

The first thing we did was to pull out our strip maps of the river, poring over the sketchy details of the banks and mileage markers, and trying to figure out how we could have miscalculated. The rapids had been among our most reliable landmarks, but now there were none. We went to sleep that night uneasy in the

Lost . . . and Found!

knowledge that we were lost. We guessed we had somewhere between thirty and forty miles to swim and food enough for a day and a half if we didn't binge.

But the next morning we again ate an enormous breakfast. After eating we totaled our remaining food: we had two cans of meat apiece, a little flour, and John had a can of peaches. Well, anyway, we were better off than Major Powell had been at this point. (He had only a few biscuits, and his party had split up.) So we put a few more pieces of driftwood into our boxes and shoved off.

It was frustrating not to know where we were. And since we had been unable to buy the last strip map in the series, we would soon have no clues whatever.

We drifted along all morning without running a single rapid. The sun was hot and the water cold, though we seemed to tolerate it a little better and took only one break that morning. Once, in mid afternoon, we came upon a side canyon very suddenly. What appeared to be a solid wall as we approached from upstream dramatically revealed the narrow crevice of a side canyon. It might have been Surprise Canyon, which was noted on our last map. But where was Surprise Rapid, also noted?

The terrain began to get lower and more open. We still saw buttes towering up thousands of feet, but they seemed set back farther from the river and there were more of them. The river, too, became wider and shallower. In its center a series of waves made it seem as if we were in one continuous rapid, or at least the tail of one. These waves were small, two or three feet high, but when we were in the troughs we could touch bottom. We had a few light moments bouncing along these waves, standing momentarily on the sand and then being pitched forward by the current. It was like bouncing along on a pogo stick.

Occasionally we came to a sand bar where we could try to stand up in the river, but as usual the current was too strong, and even though the water was only knee deep, it bowled us over. We noticed that now the silt banks were more pronounced; they generally were of uniform height, about four feet, and stretched along the shore for miles without a break.

The day and the terrain were absolutely gorgeous. John remarked, "You know, Bill, even though we've been in these canyons for over three weeks—25 days to be exact—they seem to get more beautiful and more awesome each day." I agreed.

Now that we were off our last map and did not know exactly what lay ahead, our curiosity and our impatience were insatiable. We swam on all afternoon without a break just to see what lay around each bend. The water had warmed up, at last registering the 59 degrees we had prepared for, and our rubber shirts and long johns did a fair job. But when we finally did begin to feel miserably cold, even though it took longer, it was no different than earlier.

That night we guessed we were about 25 miles from Pierce Ferry, based on the assumption that it really was Surprise Canyon we had identified. It seemed very likely that this would be our last night out. We began, like primitive men, to see omens. The first was the airplane which came buzzing up the canyon about 500 feet off the water. It signaled that we were close to civilization again. That night John drained the last of his bourbon and with a ceremonial flourish declared, "The day I go without whiskey is the day I stop."

We speculated a lot that night on what would happen when we got out of the river. How much publicity had there been about us? How much was to come? We guessed we might get a little attention for a few days. There would be a newspaper story, a magazine article or two and our movies might get on TV, but after a month everyone would forget all about it and we would be just John and Bill again. After all, we had conceived the whole thing just for fun and that was pretty much how it had stayed—the difficulties notwithstanding. We had had a lot of fun on this swim

Lost . . . and Found!

and would remember it for the rest of our lives. We considered that we might go on and do other things together, adventuresome or otherwise, but whatever did happen, this three and a half weeks would always be important to us.

In the morning came the final omen signaling that this would indeed be our last day on the river.

We were again blasted out of our sound sleep by an atom bomb!

It boomed through the canyons, echoing back and forth off the cliffs for several minutes; it sounded like the end of the world.

The bomb served to put us in the water very early. There was almost no breakfast anyway, so we were in well before we saw the sun, determined to get to Pierce Ferry even if we had to swim after dark. The river kept its new character—wider and shallower—and the silt banks grew slowly higher. Very soon they were 20 feet high, and as the river cut under them, often a section would give way with a great *whoosh*. Sometimes we would see a quarter of a mile of bank slump down while thousands of tons of silt slid back into the river, like sand glaciers calving icebergs. This was clearly part of that half-million tons of silt a day the Colorado River carried into Lake Mead.

It was obvious to us now that we were swimming in what had once been a finger of Lake Mead that stretched into the Grand Canyon during high water. The river, having reached the lake and slowed down, had dumped its silt here in the lower Grand Canyon, burying all the rapids in sand. Now the lake was again lower and the river was cutting away at the silt banks, moving them farther down into the lake.

We kept looking west, hoping at each bend in the river to see the end of the cliffs and buttes and be in open country again. Sometime around noon, after we had been swimming for several hours, I got trapped in a big whirlpool and John got about a mile ahead of me. When I looked down at the end of a long corridor he was just a little speck waving at me. Then I saw a group of buildings, a small airstrip and some strange machinery near him and realized he was stopping. When I got there John could already tell me no one was there.

This was the bat guano mine that had provided us our tent at Pierce Ferry the night we were there four weeks before. Fascinating place; they had a big vacuum tank in the middle of the camp with a half-mile long six-inch pipe leading up to a cave in the cliff. Evidently the stuff was vacuumed off the floor of the cave, put in sacks at the camp, and then flown to Pierce Ferry in a light plane. It was clearly very concentrated and valuable fertilizer to justify such expensive handling.

We were sorry there was no one we could cadge a little food from—we were down to one can of peaches between us, and had had no lunch. With sighs for lunch we hastened back into the water and around the next bend.

"Oh, son of a bitch!" we yelled. There were more cliffs and buttes ahead. We weren't out yet.

"Hey, pull over here!" came a voice.

"What did you say?" we said to each other.

"Hey, HI! Over here!"

By golly there were three people standing over on the bank. The first people we had actually seen on the edge of the river since Lees Ferry. We waved and kept on going; we were in a hurry now and really didn't want to stop. But they kept waving insistently so we agreed that they could at least tell us how far we had left to go. Besides, maybe they had an extra sandwich.

As we drew closer we could see that they were taking pictures. Taking pictures? One guy had three cameras on tripods on the bank and two hanging around his neck, and he was jumping from camera to camera like a monkey on a string. The other two guys were clicking away pretty fast, too.

When we got there these two men and a boy started congratulating us saying, "Welcome, welcome" and "Nice goin' "and a lot of stuff like that. They talked back and forth about the "historic event," and chuckled over the first words of the "intrepid swimmers" as they emerged from the Grand Canyon, telling us that, "son of a bitch!" wouldn't sound too good, so could we please say something a little more suitable to the occasion?

We were confused. We couldn't understand what they were doing here, but gathered they had heard about us from the news stories. We tried to turn the conversation away from ourselves and asked them if they'd come out here to fish.

"No, we came out to meet you."

Oh come on. *That* was a little hard to swallow. "Say, where *are* we exactly?" I asked, changing tacks.

"About five miles from Pierce Ferry—two or three miles from the Grand Wash Cliffs."

Super! We'd make it today for sure.

"Well thanks, guys. We'd better be shoving off." Something just wasn't right. The sooner we got out of here the better. "Right, John?"

"Yeah, thanks guys." We turned to the water.

"Hey, wait a minute. Let us get a few more pictures?"

A few more! Jeez, they'd taken more in ten minutes than we had in 26 days. But we agreed to pose if they would take a few movies of us. We might as well get some footage showing how happy we were at the end and all that.

Movies done, we again started to leave when this guy who seemed to be running the show, Bill Belknap, asked us to wait till he broke camp so he could follow us in his boat. We asked how long they had been camped here.

"Oh, we just got here and had just set up when you two came around the bend. We were ready to stay out a week."

John and I exchanged looks. Maybe these people weren't kidding us after all. We eased up and chatted a few minutes with them while they stowed things in their boat nearby and took some more pictures, this time of us eating that last can of peaches. Bill and his son Buzz Belknap and a Park Service man really had come up to wait for us. Bill had run the canyon several times and was one of the bona fide experts on it.

We were overwhelmed. We could hardly believe that anyone would come all the way out here just to meet us. It wasn't exactly Lindberg at Le Bourget, but we were impressed. Back in the water we bounced along the waves gaily, whooping and shouting at each other while our boat full of escorts circled around us time and again, taking pictures of us with their cameras and ours.

The silt banks had built up by this time to nearly 50 feet; and the slumping seemed to be going on continuously. I got caught in one of the vagaries of Colorado currents and was carried to within a couple of feet of a bank just upstream of a jutting peninsula of sand. I got whirled around a bit in the eddy and had just fought clear of it when the whole bank and half the peninsula came down with a roar. Sand and spray flew out and nearly blinded me. John, from his distance, was sure I had been buried.

It was the river's last shot at me.

John's last struggle was to get caught in so powerful an eddy that he couldn't swim back into the main current, no matter how hard he tried. So he climbed ashore, dragged his boxes downstream a way and got back in, only to find he hadn't gone far enough and was still in the eddy. It took him two more shots to get free. All the while Belknap's boat cruised up and down shooting movies of John struggling to swim the last mile.

We were so busy swimming we never noticed we had come out of the canyon. As the silt banks receded and the river got even wider we saw there were no more cliffs, only open, unobstructed desert sky.

It was nearly twilight when we reached the mud flat that was the Pierce Ferry landing. We'd have missed it completely without Belknap to point it out to us.

Lost . . . and Found!

And there was another surprise waiting for us. The two happiest young men in Arizona met the third happiest. The Park Service had sent a Ranger out to meet us, with instructions to camp out there till we arrived. The young man was now free to go home to his new bride.

We changed clothes there on the mud flat, threw all the driftwood out of our boxes, but found we couldn't part with our torn long johns and moldy sweatshirts that had been so important. Tired and hungry, we shouldered our gear and stumbled the three miles of mud flat and desert to my car.

There it was, ready and waiting for us, rain washed to a glisten—squatting on a flat tire. So much for heroes.

Just at sunset the tire was fixed and, as if relenting, the car started right up and we headed home. Our adventure—a high point in our lives—was over.

Aftermath

Over, that is, all but the shouting. For a few weeks we were famous. In Las Vegas, our first stop on the way to L.A., we were wined and dined by a casino and interviewed by wire services. That night on the car radio we had the odd experience of hearing about ourselves on the news. We didn't get home till dawn but already reporters and TV cameramen were waiting at our door. By the time they had left, our normally chaotic apartment was a shambles.

We never got to see or hear any of those first TV stories. The press tied us up that whole first day with interviews and phone calls. We finished at 11:30 P.M. on a TV interview show. At 6:30 the next morning the first phone call came in, followed by scores more. For days we had no time to unpack. After about a week of answering the demands made on us, we were ready to jump back in at Lees Ferry. By that time we were walking again, not limping.

The publicity tapered off, but the clamor continued for months. We got offers and suggestions from friends, cranks, opportunists, experts and fools. There were guys who would make us rich for 10 percent of the take. One wanted 50 percent! Some pretty crazy stunts were proposed for us. "Sponsors" for our next adventure cropped up. We were asked to give free talks for free meals. We got invited to parties by people we didn't know. We were even counseled not to shave off our beards, but after having the awkward experience of being recognized on the streets, we shaved them off quickly.

Mostly we kept our own counsel or listened to knowledgeable friends. We appeared on a few local and national TV shows, published a couple of magazine articles and edited our movies for a TV adventure series. We were truly astounded when we finally saw all our developed movies. Almost every shot was decent. In the final version of the film more than 80 percent of the footage we took was actually used—an extraordinary percentage considering we had no experience and no light meter. Of course the reasons were those careful instructions from experts plus our penurious hashing over every shot before the button was pushed. Our filming was pedestrian, but the amateur cinematography was carried by the subject.

The TV series, with our film as one episode, played for ten years, rerunning in some cities five and six times. We edited a longer version of the film and with the help of an agent lectured with it for a year or so, telling our story, urging people to take a Grand Canyon voyage and condemning the proposed dams.

Our poor, abused little movie camera gave up the ghost a few weeks after we got home, its parts rusted into uselessness, its lenses fogged beyond their value to repair.

Our film did pay for itself and then a little. More important was its documentation of our venture. There were those who doubted our claims, from jealousy or chauvinism. But the rapids sequences, particularly Soap Creek, Hance and Lava Falls, were indisputable. Having films of ourselves swimming through what were regarded then as the three biggest rapids on the river gave us a credibility we could have gotten no other way.

We were also vouched for by a boat party that came down the Grand Canyon a few weeks after us. They reported to Dock Marston, the river's leading historian, that they had seen our footprints at a number of rapids and that the footprints always re-entered the water at the same place they left — indicating that we had indeed not walked around those rapids.

Dock Marston invited me along on his trip the next year so I made my second trip driving a speedboat. I was impressed with how much more visibility a boatman has than a swimmer. Sitting a few feet above the water on a boat instead of floating mere inches above the surface let me see a whole rapids well before entering it. On that trip I swam through Soap Creek, Hance, Nankoweap and several others for fun, and also to demonstrate to an audience of old river runners that it could be done. I don't think some had really accepted that we had swum the whole Grand Canyon, and on my repeat swims these experts lined the banks, cameras at the ready. When we got to Lava Falls I swam it once; I enjoyed it so much I trudged back upstream and swam it a second time. All those later swims were, of course, in warm water and I was unencumbered by those boxes. For all we had used them as protection, the boxes were a nuisance and it *is* easier to swim rapids without them. However, I did wear fins and a life jacket. Not to have either in a big rapids is probably hazardous.

I think I really put it to some of the skeptics when I got half the party to take my $5 bet that I could swim across the swift Colorado and finish upstream of my starting point. In fact I did it both coming and going; the trick of course, was using those ever-present whirlpools.

Later that year John and I made a rubber raft trip with my dog, Sam, from Lees Ferry to Bright Angel to make a movie for a TV series. On that trip we each swam a rapid or two for old time's sake and did a sequence where one of us fell out of the boat at the head of a rapid. We paused at President Harding, and using our own film, reenacted John's near disaster. Sadly, that film was destroyed when again a "waterproof" rubber box leaked. Also on that trip the balky outboard motor we were given broke down finally and completely a few miles above Bright Angel. Since we had lost one oar and broken the other, John and I got in the water with our fins and life jackets and towed the hapless raft the last three or four miles while Sam barked joyously.

The next year John swam Bright Angel Rapids for a segment of ABC's "Wide World" and the year after that I was hired to be a member of the crew making a Walt Disney film dramatizing Major Powell's pioneer voyage. My job was to be the pilot of "Major Powell's boat." At one time or another I was also the double for every part in the movie except Major Powell himself. That year I wasn't so "lucky" at Bedrock Rapid. I hit the same fishhook of rock that got John and ripped a four-foot slash in Major Powell's boat. Only a quick grounding saved the boat and the movie. Bedrock has done in several other boats since and drowned one boatman. I again swam another few rapids on that trip, including Lava Falls.

It is against regulations to swim in the Colorado River in the Grand Canyon. But they tell me that every now and then someone swims through a medium-sized rapid to see what it's like. As far as I know, no one has ever attempted to duplicate our swim — certainly no one has succeeded. And now, I guess, no one would be allowed to try. Not that we set out to make some sort of record; it really was just a cheap vacation that got a little out of hand.

One of the things we have always been proud of about our swim was its influence on the popularity of the Grand Canyon voyage. According to Marston, John and I were the 219th and 220th persons ever to make a trip through the entire Grand Canyon by any method. That same year, following us, that number more than doubled. Before we swam it, the voyage was regarded as dangerous—not for an ordinary tourist. We were not the first to debunk that myth, but the enormous amount of publicity we received, and the dramatic facts of our trip, caused people to say, "It can't be that dangerous, two guys swam it." Soon thousands per year began seeing the Grand Canyon by river—over 14,000 one year.

I have always wished this one small contribution of ours had not been overlooked.

We've always lived with the fact that many considered our swim to be only a stunt. To this day the echoes of those headlines, the film lectures that followed and the ten years of reruns of the TV episode still conspire to stick a label on us which has never completely faded. We are still approached now and then by somebody who says, "Say, aren't you one of those two crazy guys who . . . . "

In 1985, some 30 years after our swim, my two children, curious about their Dad's adventure, convinced me to take them on a commercial raft trip through the Grand Canyon. I was both surprised and flattered at the attention given me by the professional river guides—embarrassed even, when one of them said to me, "You know, you guys are still real legends on this river." He showed me that our swim was given a paragraph or so in half a dozen books on Grand Canyon history. And I again found myself answering the same barrages of questions I thought long forgotten. I was even asked to give a campfire talk.

When I got home to the Virgin Islands, at the urging of my children, I dug out the old notes, photos and half-completed manuscript buried in the dust of our storeroom and wrote this book. It was as fun reliving our swim, as the original swim itself had been.

But my feelings were confused by that return trip to the river. At first, I was a little depressed by some of the changes I saw.

No longer were the shorelines swept clean by annual floods. Now the tamarisk, a dirty little shrub from the Far East, unmolested by floods, cluttered up many of the remaining campsites. The great silt banks were gone, along with the jelly-like mud flats. There were no fascinating acres of driftwood piled up on shore or floating in eddies. The water released in controlled amounts from Glen Canyon Dam, the cause of all these changes, at first was clear, the silt left in Lake Powell behind the dam. I could easily see those submerged rocks we guessed at in Soap Creek and in some of the earlier rapids. However, before we got to the mouth of the Little Colorado the water was again opaque, and by the Grand Wash cliffs the busy brown Colorado was carrying its traditional heavy load of silt.

Another effect of that dam is that the water released is from the bottom of the lake and is cold. Very cold. Down to 50 degrees. I refused to swim again at all in the Colorado, even in calm water. After 30 years the memory still lingered.

John and I were the only two people on the river during our swim, and the vagaries of current meant that we spent the greater part of each day swimming alone. The Grand Canyon is a very big place to be alone and that total solitude was one of the aesthetic blessings of our trip. On a boat trip today one encounters many, many other parties afloat and ashore and one is never alone. The usual price of popularity. Pity one can't have both.

It's ironic that Glen Canyon Dam, which most river devotees consider an abomination for drowning lovely Glen Canyon and neutering the Colorado, should be located only a few miles from the most productive uranium mines in the U.S. I've always fancied that a nuclear power plant tucked into a deep, lonely side canyon could have produced the same electricity as That Dam and saved the canyons as well. Would have made the water a little warmer, too.

But returning to the Canyon after more than a third of a million canyon voyagers, I was delighted by the changes that *hadn't* taken place. Marble Canyon, the Grand Canyon and the many

Aftermath

side canyons are as beautiful as ever. And considering that some of the old cables and other wreckage that we saw on the swim have been taken away, there is today even less of man's debris in the Canyon than 30 years ago.

Somehow the Park Service, the dedicated professionals, and the general enthusiasm of the public for keeping the environment pristine have performed wonders along the Colorado River. Save for our sidetrips, John and I never saw another's footprints, now they are everywhere—but that's all.

Everything taken into the canyon is removed, including human wastes, which are carried out in oversized porta-potties. No one makes fires on the ground to leave dirty ashes for the next party—instead river voyagers make their fires in special steel boxes and take the ashes out with them. Our group searched for and removed every speck of stray litter each morning before departure and obviously our predecessors had done the same.

The Park Service limits the number of people and the number of days they can spend on river trips. This rationing has inevitably increased competition for space. It is now a several-year wait for one of the rare non-commercial permits to make a river voyage.

Consequently, squabbling has arisen in recent years over the use of the Grand Canyon. Various groups claiming a special relationship with the place are busily trying to restrict Canyon usage by other groups.

In the mid 80s, oar-powered boat lovers fenced off three months of the year for their exclusive use. Motorized boats got no such privilege. Hikers now are censured for leaving nearly permanent trail scars on a fragile desert landscape. And none of these groups welcomes tourists seeing the Grand Canyon from helicopters or other aircraft.

If boaters and hikers resent aircraft noise, the clutter of boats and trails equally offends airplane passengers who can claim to be the best conservationists of all—they neither leave any trace nor upset animals (who have no evolutionary fear of engines). Why not a time or place when only airplanes are allowed?

And as campsites diminish with the silt banks, why can't the compact motorized trips have three months for *their* exclusive use?

Of course, as some are suggesting, we could turn the Grand Canyon into a super wilderness area and allow no conveyances whatever. Then we could restrict canyon trips to . . . swimmers?

Silly? No sillier than some of the things you can hear.

Because of this silly debate I have come to admire the men and women of the Park Service for the way they deal with every kind of advocate, from selfish "environmentalists" to selfish "exploiters" (sometimes interchangeable). Somehow, despite a few errors, they still manage to let the Parks be for all the people without letting the Parks become too overrun. The Park Service contends with changing political winds—local and national—with its own ignorance and others', with emotions, stupidity, foolhardiness, fads, and plain greed. Considering all this, I sometimes think the Park Service performs miracles. I certainly forgive them their mistakes.

That they have been able to see to it that the banks of the Colorado are kept unspoiled without resorting to a paid patrolman on every trip or at every campsite is a tribute to the Park Service. Most other bureaucracies would have seized such an opportunity to expand their empire, crying to Congress for millions more to "keep the Canyon clean." Today's Park Service is wise enough to see that cooperation is better than coercion, and just as our Kindly Old Superintendent had the courage to let us go on, knowing full well the consequences if he had been wrong, so today's Park Service personnel seem to be able to trust the innate wisdom of most members of the public.

I rediscovered on my last voyage that the Canyon still grips its travelers in its mysticism. No one is cynical or matter-of-fact

Aftermath

about the Grand Canyon. It is perhaps the world's greatest natural wonder. There is so much in the experience of being down in it that cannot be grasped. Its size, its age, its power, its beauty are so grand, so completely overwhelming, so beyond comprehension that the human brain is overpowered, numbed. Previous perspectives are reoriented, experiences negated, conclusions doubted.

The Canyon becomes a mind altering drug, the canyoneer an addict. He wonders if ordinary people can understand what he's experienced; he becomes "born again," sharing a bond only with others of the same persuasion. It becomes "his" or "her" canyon.

Only the initiated can truly understand the power of this fanatic possessiveness.

I easily see why some try to make the Canyon their exclusive preserve. I understand their feelings, I share their addiction, but I protest — even though my life has been more profoundly affected by the Grand Canyon that most people's lives have been.

It does, after all, belong to all of us.

THE AUTHOR, now a resident of St. Thomas, Virgin Islands, went on the lecture circuit with the Grand Canyon film following the venture. Later he became a reporter for newspapers and TV, did some script writing and producing and public relations work, and finally bought a schooner and settled in St. Thomas where he runs charters and a boatyard. His schooner *True Love* had a starring role in the Bing Crosby movie "High Society," giving rise to the hit song of the same name.

Other books from The Mountaineers include:

MILES FROM NOWHERE: A Round-the-World Bicycle Adventure
By Barbara Savage. Best-selling account of the Savages' two-year, 23,000-mile, 25-country tour, as heard on NPR's "Radio Reader."

KEEP IT MOVING: Baja by Canoe
By Valerie Fons. Narrative of a 2,411-mile journey around the Baja Peninsula by canoe; a compelling story of personal growth and partnership.

EVEREST GRAND CIRCLE: A Climbing and Skiing Adventure Through Nepal and Tibet
By Ned Gillette, Jan Reynolds. First circumnavigation of Everest, plus climb of 23,442-foot Pumori in winter, travel in hostile, uncharted terrain where few Westerners had been.

MOMENTS OF DOUBT and Other Mountaineering Writings of David Roberts
Collection of 20 essays and articles on mountaineering and adventure, selected from Roberts' work of two decades. " . . . most perceptive American writer on mountaineering today."—New York Times

AN INNOCENT ON THE MIDDLE FORK
By Eliot DuBois. Engaging story of first solo kayak run down Middle Fork of Idaho's Salmon River.

MANY PEOPLE COME, LOOKING, LOOKING
By Galen Rowell. From the springboard of three Himalayan climbing trips, Rowell traces the changes in lives and culture of Himalayan peoples since their countries opened to trekkers and mountaineers. " . . . an armchair explorer's Nirvana."—Los Angeles Times

Write for illustrated catalog of more than 100 outdoor titles:

**The Mountaineers
306 Second Avenue W., Seattle WA 98119**